BAD PETS

BAD to the BONE

ALLAN ZULLO

Scholastic Inc.

To Linda and Cheryl Hill, whose love of animals is matched only
by their fondness for fun.
—A.Z.

ISBN 978-1-338-26361-9

10 9 8 7 6   22 23

Printed in the U.S.A.   40
First printing 2019

CONTENTS

WILD KINGDOM

The animal world is one wild kingdom.

Whether they live in a doghouse or a birdcage, roam in a neighborhood or a forest, play in the backyard or the family room, pets and wild creatures often turn into mischief-makers, troublemakers, and noisemakers.

Some of their wackiest escapades have been documented in *Bad Pets: True Tales of Misbehaving Animals*; *Bad Pets on the Loose!*; *Bad Pets Most Wanted!*; and *Bad Pets Hall of Shame*. But four books can't come close to covering all the silliness and naughtiness of family pets and wild animals. So this book offers another fun collection of true accounts of animal shenanigans ranging from the bizarre to the ridiculous.

For example, you will read about the dog who

brought a gushing water sprinkler into the house, the pet goat who stole candy from a convenience store, the dogs who sank their owners' cars, the possum who got drunk in a liquor store, the donkeys who wound up in jail, the dog who destroyed a wedding cake on the day of the big event, the cow who got stuck between two trees, and the cats who took unwanted spins in the family dryers.

One thing is certain: Cats and dogs, cows and bulls, goats and sheep, and other animals both wild and domesticated make the animal kingdom one silly, goofy, zany world.

THIEVES

A KID IN A CANDY STORE

Daisy the goat had a sweet disposition—perhaps too sweet. It led her to steal candy from a convenience store.

After tying her up outside a 7-Eleven store in Tigard, Oregon, on a chilly winter day in 2017, her owner went inside. But Daisy wanted to join him, so she managed to free herself and then waited for her opportunity. That's when customer Katelyn Lund approached the store's front entrance.

"When I opened the doors, she was pretty adamant about going in and went past me," Lund told the *Oregonian*. "And, honestly, I didn't know how to handle a goat, so I just let her in." A thankful Daisy hoofed it straight for the aisle that showcased candy.

Lund looked around to see if a clerk or shopper considered anything odd about a goat studying the array of sugary treats. But no one else in the store was paying any attention to the goat. "Everyone was nonchalant about her, and no one said anything to her," Lund recalled. "At that point I'm thinking, 'Dude, does no one realize that there's a real live goat in here? And where's your mom?'"

Daisy made her choice. She pulled a package of Sour Skittles off the shelf and began munching on the candy while Lund recorded the theft on her cell phone. Lund posted a photo and video of Daisy on Facebook, commenting, "If anyone in the Portland area is looking for their goat, she's eating Sour Skittles at the 7-Eleven on Scholls Ferry."

Daisy obviously had a sweet tooth, judging by the candy she was eating. "You should know she's not just about the Skittles," Lund said. "Ol' girl was pulling down all types of candy." She added that Daisy "was working on a Snickers bar" when Lund left the store.

"It turns out the guy checking out right next to me was her owner," she said. He stopped the thievery before it *goat* out of hand.

CANINE CAPER

The cops in Shafter, California, were dogged by a cute Siberian husky they dubbed the Bread Bandit after she pulled off a *crumb-y* heist. Security cameras at a dollar store showed her snatching a loaf of bread right off a shelf and then fleeing.

"This dog came in and she was really friendly, looking around," employee Abby Lopez told Bakersfield TV station KGET. No one suspected that the pleasant pooch had a devious scheme in mind. The husky went over to the shelf that held loaves of Wonder Bread and must have thought that this was the greatest thing since, well, sliced bread. "The next thing we know," Lopez said, "she grabs a loaf and starts running around" while an employee gave chase.

At the entrance to the store, the worker caught up to the crook and tried to detain her by gripping her tail and spinning her around. When the husky refused to let go of the loaf, the two engaged in a brief tug-of-war. The dog clearly was the breadwinner, leaving the employee holding a torn piece of plastic wrap and a few crushed slices. The culprit then disappeared into the evening, figuring a half a loaf was better than none at all.

Because a crime had been committed, the cops were

called. The Shafter Police Department posted surveillance footage of the pilfering pooch on Facebook, saying, "On May 17th, 2017, at approximately 9:20 p.m., the suspect in this video entered the Dollar General on Lerdo Hwy. and shoplifted a loaf of bread. The suspect was able to avoid apprehension and escaped on all fours out the front doors. The suspect is described as a white and gray husky last seen carrying a loaf of bread. Any information is appreciated, as she looks hungry."

During a search of the immediate area, Officer Nick Riddick, Shafter's animal control manager, found pieces of the stolen bread in an alleyway behind the Dollar General. Because there were no other clues, it looked like this would remain an unsolved crime. Riddick's only hope: "Crooks end up getting greedy, which is why they get caught," he said.

Doggone if that husky didn't get greedy. She returned to the scene of the crime the next day—with an accomplice! Her partner was another female husky like her, only brown and white.

This time, their plan went *a-rye*, and they both got collared. The accomplice was nabbed right in front of the store, while the Bread Bandit was captured about a block away.

Rather than put up a fight, they each wagged their tails and licked their captors' hands. Because the dogs had no tags or embedded chips, they were locked up in the Shafter Critters Shelter while authorities waited for any possible owners to claim their canine criminals.

The story and photos of the huskies' heist went viral. Two days later, owners of the accomplice came forward and bailed out their pet, whose name was Bella.

Surprisingly, the two dogs hadn't known each other before they slipped away from their owners. Somehow, they teamed up on the streets of Shafter, looking for trouble. "It's the most bizarre thing," Riddick told the *New York Post.* "I've been in animal control for nine years now, and this is the first time I've come across conspiratorial canines. I don't know how they hooked up. They were completely friendly and were the sweetest of pals." Referring to a classic film of two women on the run from the law, he added, "They were like buddies out on a crime spree, like Thelma and Louise."

Because so many people claimed they were the Bread Bandit's owner or wanted to adopt her, officials decided the dog would be better off in another town, city project manager Brittney Neal-Soberanis said. The husky was turned over to Recycled Pets NorCal, of Roseville, California, which found her a new, loving family. In a nod to Victor Hugo's classic novel, *Les Misérables,* about a man who was imprisoned for stealing a loaf of bread, the dog received a new name: Jean Valjean.

Don the border collie stole an all-terrain vehicle and turned it into a *wreck-reational* vehicle by driving it through a fence and across two lanes of traffic during the morning rush hour and then crashing into a barrier.

Before all this craziness, which happened in 2015, Don was riding beside 77-year-old farmer Tom Hamilton, who was operating his Gator all-terrain vehicle (ATV) in a field near Abington, South Lanarkshire, Scotland. Hamilton told BBC Scotland that they motored onto a field where he planned to check on several lambs that were grazing near a busy highway known as the M74 motorway.

Hamilton stopped at the top of a steep hill. Forgetting to set the brake, he got out to examine a lamb. He assumed Don, who had ridden with him for years without any trouble, would stay put in the Gator. But the four-year-old brown-and-white dog decided to take it for a joyride.

Don hopped from the passenger's seat to the driver's seat and leaned on the controls. With the dog happily planted on the seat, the ATV crept forward and then picked up speed as it rumbled down the hill toward a fence at the bottom of an embankment.

"I was sorting out one of the lambs," Hamilton

recalled. "When I turned around to get back in the tractor, it was going down the hill and heading toward the motorway. I ran after it, but I couldn't catch up. I can't really run very fast, and I ended up falling over. I thought the fence would have stopped him, but it didn't."

Don remained in the Gator as it smashed through the fence that paralleled the bustling road. Despite the impact, which cracked the windshield, Don refused to jump off. Instead, he rode across two lanes of northbound traffic before crashing the Gator into a barrier in the median.

"I was just hoping Don was going to be all right and that the tractor wouldn't hit any of the cars or that they wouldn't hit him," Hamilton said. "It was very busy at the time, so I was worried."

Startled drivers had managed to swerve and brake to avoid striking Don and the Gator. The dog, who was unhurt but confused by his *faux paw*, waited in the Gator until his relieved owner arrived. Minutes later, the police showed up. Traffic began to slow down when passing rubberneckers tried to process what they were seeing because it all seemed so *fur-fetched*.

Traffic Scotland, which gives reports to motorists, tweeted that there was a traffic jam "due to dog taking control of tractor . . . nope, not joking. Farmer & police at scene." Afterward, Traffic Scotland tweeted, "Route is clear from earlier incident, and dog is fine. Has to be the weirdest thing we have ever reported!"

Hamilton told the BBC Scotland, "It's terrible. But people seem to find it amusing. I'm just glad Don didn't cause an accident. I can't believe no one was injured. We've all been very lucky. But I think his driving days are over." Yes, Don has been *cur-tailed*.

FOR THE BIRDS

Seagulls are notorious thieves. They always seem to have a bold plan they can carry off.

For example, a nasty seagull swooped down on an unsuspecting man who was paying for a pizza and flew off with his wallet.

On a summer evening in downtown Gloucester, Massachusetts, in 2018, Brian Fines, of Rhode Island, had placed his billfold on the top of a box containing a pizza he had just purchased. Suddenly, out of the dusk, a seagull appeared. Gulls are known for stealing food such as ice-cream cones, sandwiches, and French fries from the hands of victims. But this flying fiend was after Fines's money.

Before the startled human victim could react, the gull zoomed low and swiped the wallet in its beak and took off. Fortunately, witnesses saw the bandit fly over a building on Main Street and drop the billfold onto the roof. The culprit then disappeared into the twilight.

Fines approached a police officer and told him his feathered *tail* of woe. The officer approached Phil Peterson, who was nearby using a cherry picker to hang lights. When he heard what had happened, Peterson thought it was "completely ridiculous and had no idea that it was a true story," he told New England Cable News (NECN). "The officer was laughing and said, 'You can't make up this stuff.'"

Peterson, along with another worker, Mike Ramos, used the cherry picker to access the flat roof. "There were two baby seagulls right there literally trying to eat the wallet," Peterson told NECN. He tried to distract the fledgling criminals by throwing bread near them. Like their partner in crime, however, they weren't interested in food. Instead, the angry birds assaulted Peterson.

"It was like the movie *The Birds*," said Peterson, referring to the classic 1963 film about thousands of birds attacking people. "I was afraid they were going to pick my brains."

Ramos, who had borrowed a flashlight from the police officer, tried to distract the birds. "I took the strobe part of the flashlight and every time the gulls tried to go after him, I would shine it at them and it would discombobulate them," Ramos told NECN. The strobe light confused the birds and kept them away from the wallet, allowing Peterson just enough time to pick it up. Then the two men hopped into the bucket of the cherry picker and returned to the ground in triumph.

"There's a whole crowd at that time, and they're giving him the thumbs-up, and it was just the craziest thing I ever saw in my life," Ramos said.

No wonder *gull* is a *four-letter bird*.

A seagull seized a new iPhone that recorded the entire crime.

In 2016, Chloe Rainey, 23, of Tiverton, Devon, England, was at nearby Exmouth Beach, where she planned to video herself and a friend sprinting up and down seaside stairs for her blog about running.

"The beach was deserted," Rainey told the *Daily Mail*. "There was nobody around so we set up the video to post to the blog. I put my brand new phone down on my jumper [sweater] on the beach and started filming, and off we went."

In the video, which she posted to Facebook, Rainey and her friend are running up and down the steps of a seawall about 30 yards away. Seconds later, the seagull appears in the shot, waddling over to the sweater. Rainey sees the winged crook and shouts, "Hey, you seagull, don't you go stealing my phone!"

Rainey recalled, "The next thing I knew, I saw the seagull circling my jumper and then it grabbed my phone. I started shouting and ran back, but the seagull wouldn't let go. I was gobsmacked [shocked]. I had to swipe at it with my jumper for it to let go."

The video shows the culprit seizing the phone with its beak and then running down the beach. The phone captures the gull's webbed feet kicking up sand before the bird goes airborne. Only after Rainey whacks the thief with her sweater does the gull drop the phone and fly off.

"The whole thing was hilarious, really," she said.

That bird showed a lot of *gull* trying to steal her phone.

MAKING A BIG SPLASH

For a fun-loving dog, there's nothing like a plunge into the water . . . unless the plunge involves a car that the pooch was taking for a joyride.

For example, Rosie, a three-month-old German shepherd, wound up way over her head when she tried her paw at driving. In 2014, the frisky pup was on a retractable leash held by her owner John Costello as they walked along Bolivar Pond in Canton, Massachusetts. At the end of their walk, they got into a Dodge Neon.

Costello had just started the car, when Rosie tried

to take over. "The dog jumped and hit the gear shift, and the car jerked," Costello told Boston TV station WFXT. "Then she fell on top of the gas pedal."

And the car took off—right into the water. "It was just scary," Costello said. "The car went for a swim. We all did."

When the car first splashed into the pond, Costello leaped out and tried to grab the dog, but he couldn't reach her. The vehicle slid farther and deeper into the water, shoving the door closed and trapping the pup. Realizing that driving was definitely not a dog thing, Rosie jumped into the back seat.

By now, the car was about 30 feet out into the pond. Eric Hermann, who was working nearby, and an unidentified man rushed to help Costello save Rosie. "The puppy was scared," Hermann told WFXT. The men were trying to coax her to jump out of the rear open window, because the back seat was filling up with water, but she was too afraid.

"I just leaped in and grabbed the dog and pulled her out, and we both fell back into the water," said Costello.

The water level soon rose over the men's heads. "By the time we got the puppy out, the car had slid and we had to do a little swimming," Hermann said.

But they all made it safely to shore. "I'm glad they were there because if they weren't, I don't know what I would have done," said Costello, who called 911 after returning to shore.

"I've never heard of a puppy driving a car into a pond," said Officer Robert Quirk of the Canton Police Department. The department later tweeted a photo of the waterlogged Rosie with the caption, "Perp says she was just going with the flow of traffic."

The car, which belonged to Costello's daughter, was pulled out of the pond. The insurance company determined it was a total loss.

Costello told CNN that he wouldn't punish Rosie. "She's very hyper, energetic, and a troublemaker, but there's no jail time for this puppy. Just plenty of hugs and kisses—and no more driving."

Too bad Rosie didn't learn from the experience of Charlie, a black Labrador retriever, who stole his owner's car and sent it into the Pend Oreille River.

The dog's owner, Mark Ewing, of Sagle, Idaho, arrived at his waterfront home and parked his Chevrolet Impala in the driveway one evening in 2007. Ewing was walking toward the front door when Charlie gave him a happy greeting and then leaped into the car through the open driver's-side window. The dog was always looking for a chance to go for a ride. But it was dinnertime, and Ewing had brought home a pizza.

Well, if Charlie couldn't get his master to drive him, maybe the dog would just have to drive himself.

"He somehow got the car into neutral," Ewing told the Spokane, Washington, newspaper *Spokesman-Review*. "My car just went down an incline and into the drink."

Seconds before the car splashed into the river and settled to the bottom, Charlie bailed out through the window. Ewing's son kayaked to the sunken car, which was a total loss, to retrieve golf clubs and other items.

"There's nothing weirder than looking at your car cruising down your driveway when you're not in it and seeing your dog jump out, and then watching your car go splash," Ewing told the newspaper. Charlie was fine. After police arrived, Ewing gave them a *Lab report*.

UNDER(WEAR) SUSPICION

For more than a year, no one in a New Zealand neighborhood could figure out why their undies were missing, until they discovered they were targeted by a cat burglar—a feisty feline named Mo.

Ed Williams of Mount Eden, a suburb of Auckland, was perplexed when ladies' underwear began showing up at the foot of his bed and in his backyard garden. Within a few weeks, he had a box full of clothes—mostly men's and women's undies—that didn't belong to him or his girlfriend. Neighbors reported that certain personal clothing items were missing, and they began to worry that a creepy crook was sneaking into their homes at night.

Well, they were right. Only the offender wasn't a person but Mo, a cute black-and-white Puss in Boots. Williams and his girlfriend caught his pet in the act of committing a theft. "We saw Mo run across the road with a T-shirt in his mouth," Williams told the *New Zealand Herald*. "We put two and two together, and that it was actually Mo bringing all the clothes over."

The cat's under(wear)taking wasn't brief. During a two-year period, Mo had slipped into open windows or cat flaps to pilfer undies and other items, enough to fill five large boxes. "Our cat is literally mental," Williams posted on Facebook in 2017 with photos of Mo's haul. "Instead of bringing back dead birds, mice, and other wildlife, Mo decides to bring home underwear and clothing, stolen from the neighbors' washing lines. This is the THIRD haul of this size so far, and growing by the day."

Williams curbed his cat by keeping him home. Thinking his pet's thieving days were over after four months of house arrest, Williams allowed Mo his neighborhood strolls. Sure enough, undies and other clothing items began showing up at the house. Mo's stash included Calvin Klein underwear, T-shirts, pants, socks, and undies.

In January 2018, Williams, who called his cat the "king of underwear thievery," posted a photo on Facebook of dozens of items that Mo had stolen. He wrote: "It's been a busy month for my cat Mo! This is now the FIFTH boxload of clothing he's retrieved from the local neighborhood . . . I think he's actually getting better at this!!? (To my neighbors, if u see any of your clothing here, please pop around and collect it, as I literally have no idea where it all comes from . . . But I'm sure some will be yours. Apologies for the inconvenience, but it is funny, innit?)"

Not every victim laughed off Mo's crime spree. Some residents had a *cat-niption* fit and showed up at Williams's door complaining about the *purr-petrator*. "The neighbors are a bit annoyed," Williams told the *Herald*. "We've had a couple of people come around fairly irate. But they've grown to love him after two years—although they still have to chase him off their property." *Meowtrageous*!

LION THROUGH HER TEETH

A lioness had muscles of *steal* when she ran off with a video camera belonging to a documentary film crew.

18

She must have felt much pride because she was recording the entire heist.

The producers of *My Africa*, which chronicles the lives of residents at an elephant sanctuary in Kenya for Conservation International, had set up several cameras on tripods in a field, hoping to catch footage of lions. In 2018, the crew obtained some dramatic footage—although it wasn't exactly what they had in mind.

With the crew sitting in a nearby truck, several lions approached the cameras, which were rolling. One curious lioness warily walked over to a camera that was filming her. She enjoyed her close-up so much that she snatched the camera with her jaws. As the device continued to record, the big cat ran off with the camera, its tripod, and a battery pack.

Surprised by her bold theft, the crew chased after the thief in their truck. They yelled and whistled at her, but she didn't stop, and neither did her accomplices who followed her.

"The more we chase them, the more they'll run," one of the producers said during the pursuit.

At one point, the lioness dropped the equipment. As the camera continued to record the crime, she began pulling away pieces of the gear. She finally settled on the battery pack and trotted off with the lion's share. But before the crew could retrieve the rest of the equipment, another lioness came over and picked up the camera and tripod and started dragging it off.

If the *mane* goal of the lionesses was to star in a crime movie, they succeeded.

Another lioness was not camera shy about being photographed in the act of stealing.

In 2012, Atlanta photographer Ed Hetherington was in Zimbabwe, where he set up a camera on a tripod next to a dead buffalo, hoping to get pictures of lions eating their prey. When the lions showed up, the photographer and his wife and tour guide assumed the beasts would ignore the camera and gorge themselves on the fresh kill. But rather than the game, one bold lioness went for the fame of being a thief.

"She kind of walked up to the camera, gave it a sniff or two, and picked it up," Hetherington told the New York *Daily News*. The lioness lifted the expensive equipment off its tripod and crept away, carrying it between her teeth like she would a cub. "She definitely wasn't trying to destroy it," the photographer said. "She kind of held it like she was proud of herself, almost as if she was showing it to us.'"

The lioness didn't take full advantage of the photo op because she dropped the camera about 20 seconds later, he said. Fortunately, the camera wasn't destroyed, although it was somewhat damaged.

Hetherington managed to capture the crime on another camera and used the photos to raise money for National Geographic Society's Big Cats Initiative. Yep, she sure was a *dandy lion*.

INTRUDERS

WEDDING CRASHER

Snoop the mutt made sure that a wedding had a lot of *marry-ment* when he barged into the ceremony and plopped down right on the bride's gown.

Before Snoop became Snoop, he was a nameless, lonely, stray dog in Laranjal Paulista, Sao Paulo, Brazil, searching for a friendly face. One stormy day in 2017, the rain-soaked, muddy-pawed pooch sought shelter in a tent where people were gathering for the wedding of Marília Pieroni and Matheus Gomes Martins. Because the stray wasn't on the invite list, he was ushered out. But sensing lots of love inside, he made another attempt at witnessing the nuptials.

"As the ceremony started, to everyone's surprise, the dog came in again, this time when the bridal chorus began to play," Marília told the Dodo, a website focusing on animals. Trying to be firm but gentle, several guests coaxed the wedding crasher to leave. Once he was outside, everyone assumed there would be no more interruptions.

The ceremony continued with the bride and groom standing side by side. As they exchanged their vows, who should come into the tent for the third time—none other than the wet, weary intruder.

"The dog entered and laid down to sleep right on my veil," Marília recalled. "It was a very pleasant surprise for me, because I love animals. I liked it very much." She had no problem sharing the spotlight and some of her lovely gown with the exhausted mutt. A photo of him sleeping on her veil soon went viral. "I thought the little guy was really cute," Marília told the news website HuffPost.

After seeing the bride's tender reaction, no one had the heart to shove the dog back out into the storm. At Marília's request, the dog was allowed to stay for the rest of the evening, although he did have to get off her veil and move to another spot, where he was given food and several pats on the head. During the reception, which was held under the same tent, the dog slipped away without anyone noticing. When the party broke up, no one could find the dog.

On their wedding night, Marília and Matheus made a joint decision: They would make the intruder their pet—if only they could locate him. They asked people in town to be on the lookout for the street dog. A week later, Marília received a call from a woman who spotted the four-legged vagrant. Marília rushed to the area. To her great joy, she found the missing dog and brought him home.

They named him Snoop. "He came home, and I showered him," she said. "He played a lot, ate, and drank water. He was very happy and slept super good the first night."

She told the HuffPost, "[Snoop] is adapting very well to his new routine. He is very playful, needy, and caring. We are so happy with him."

For the couple and the dog, it was a *pawsitive* outcome.

DRINKING PROBLEM

A wild possum found itself in good spirits, which led to a bad hangover after breaking into a liquor store and lapping up an entire bottle of booze.

The juvenile female critter had sneaked into Cash's Liquor Store on Okaloosa Island, Florida, one night in 2017 while the place was closed. "She came in from the outside and was up in the rafters," store owner Cash Moore told the *Northwest Florida Daily News*. "When she came through, she knocked a bottle of liquor off the shelf. When she got down on the floor, she drank the whole darn bottle." That was a pretty *whiskey* thing to do.

The next morning when an employee opened the store, he was stunned to see a drunken, passed-out possum lying next to a broken, empty bottle of bourbon. There was no puddle of booze because she had licked all of it off the floor. He didn't know if she was dead or just playing possum. A closer look showed that this "Drinkerbelle" was alive but had drunk herself under the table, which wasn't a good thing, especially considering she was under the drinking age.

The potted possum was brought to the Emerald Coast Wildlife Refuge for treatment, where she failed a sobriety test. "We looked her over, and she definitely wasn't fully acting normal," Michelle Pettis, a wildlife health technician at the refuge, told the newspaper. She said the possum appeared disoriented, was excessively salivating, and looked pale.

The staff pumped the marsupial full of fluids and cared for her as she sobered up. "We loaded her with fluids to help flush out any alcohol toxins," Pettis said. "She was good a couple of days later and was released."

Pettis added that it was the first time the staff had treated a drunken possum.

NEWS BREAKERS

Animals love to steal the limelight during live telecasts.

TV anchorman Kudret Celebioglu knows all about that. He was at his desk delivering the news on *Good Morning Denizli* on station DRT in Denizli, Turkey, in 2016, when he caught a glimpse of something furry out of the corner of his eye. A gray-and-white kitten had jumped up onto a chair next to the broadcaster, although the feline was still unseen by the audience at home. Celebioglu continued with the news as if nothing had happened.

Moments later, viewers saw two paws appear on the desk. Then the feline stuck his head up so everyone at home could see whose paws they were. After looking around, he hopped up onto the desk, distracting the anchorman, who *pawsed* for a few seconds because the cat got his tongue (figuratively speaking, of course).

Deciding the show must go on, Celebioglu announced, "We have a surprise guest in the studio." Then he continued giving the news. But that became harder when the cat wandered across the desk and turned and looked straight at the camera, hoping that it captured his good side.

Next, the intruder sauntered over to the open laptop that sat on the desk in front of Celebioglu and plopped down right on the keyboard, probably hoping for some screenshots. The newscaster kept going, at least briefly. Unable to ignore the visitor any longer, he said, "As the weather has turned colder, stray cats are getting hungry and obviously looking for places to stay warm—like in the studio. If you see a stray on the street, maybe you could feed it or take it inside."

After petting the four-legged guest on the head, Celebioglu felt the intruder had *crossed the feline* with all this attention-seeking. The anchorman asked for help from a production assistant, who then removed the stray so the news could continue without any distractions.

The cat became an instant social media star. Best of all, he was adopted by a station staff member, who gave him a new name—Hüsnü. It means "handsome man" in Turkish.

A black Labrador retriever interrupted a live Russian TV news broadcast when he sought some affection from the shocked anchorwoman.

Ilona Linarte, from Mir24-TV, was delivering a report about a Moscow demolition when she, along with viewers at home, heard a dog bark. Linarte jerked from surprise and then looked down and gasped, "Aiyee!" Viewers could see the tip of a black tail wagging furiously a few inches above the anchor desk. The dog barked again, and Linarte jumped again.

"I've got a dog here," said Linarte, looking both bewildered and amused. She tried to go on with her report, but then the Lab put his paws on her desk and sniffed her papers as if he wanted to deliver the news. His tail was still wagging.

Leaning away from the intruder, Linarte shouted to the off-screen crew, "What is this dog doing in the studio?"

What she didn't know was that the dog belonged to a guest who was slated to appear later on the program on another segment. The canine had managed to get loose and was seeking the anchorwoman's attention. Linarte patted the dog on the head and, facing the camera, confessed, "I actually prefer cats. Yeah, I'm a cat lady."

GOING ALONG FOR THE RIDE

Animals can't thumb for a ride, so they have to resort to other measures to get from here to there.

For instance, Poppy the pygmy goat wanted to take the bus, but she wasn't willing to pay her *fare* share.

The pet goat lived in a pen in a suburb of Portland, Oregon. One evening in 2008, she noticed the gate was unlatched, so she took it as an invitation to explore the neighborhood.

Around the same time, a TriMet city bus was parked nearby at a busy intersection during a layover. The bus driver had stepped outside and left the door open. Poppy ambled around the corner and spotted the bus. Perhaps wanting to see more of the city on wheels than on hooves, Poppy climbed into the bus before the startled driver could stop her.

The passengers found it funny. The driver didn't want to kick Poppy off the bus, for her own safety. He was afraid she could get either injured or killed, or cause an accident in the street or on the nearby freeway. He alerted TriMet dispatchers, who called 911. "I've got a very strange request," the caller told the emergency dispatcher. "A goat is on our bus. We need her off."

A Portland police officer arrived but couldn't find any identification on her, so he took the 35-pound black goat to a Multnomah County Animal Services shelter, where Poppy made friends with the staff.

Poppy then had her 15 minutes of fame. An animal control official told reporters that the goat had been "taken into custody by transit police for lack of proper bus fare." TriMet police spread the word that "an unauthorized kid" had been removed from the bus.

Although the local media was having fun with the bus-riding goat, her owner was worried about her lost pet. The owner, a woman who didn't want her name used, posted an ad on Craigslist, pleading for help in finding Poppy, writing, "Lost: Pygmy Goat (I-205 at Foster). My little black pygmy goat figured out how to open the gate last night and got out of the yard. She was a birthday gift, and I am really worried about her. PLEASE, if you have found or have seen her, let me know. Thank you." By later that afternoon, Poppy had been reunited with her owner. The *baaaad* day had turned into a *goat* one.

Odi the wire-haired terrier took a ride on a passenger train without a ticket and ended his trip in the slammer.

The adventurous 10-year-old pooch sneaked out of his house in Portarlington, Ireland, one morning in 2016 and then climbed aboard a commuter train bound for Dublin. A conductor didn't spot him until after the train was under way. When Odi, who was sitting in an unoccupied seat, couldn't produce a ticket, he was considered a stowaway, but he was allowed to stay on the train for the 90-minute ride to the station in Dublin.

The conductor took a photo of the dog, which was posted on Irish Rail's Facebook page with the message, "If this is your doggie, please contact Kilmainham Garda Station."

After the train pulled into Dublin, Odi was taken to an animal shelter and locked up over the weekend.

Odi's owner, Siobhan Mulligan, told the *Irish Independent* that because the shelter was closed, she had to wait until Monday to pick up her stray mutt. Then she had to pay a fee of about $140. "We don't mind at all," she told the newspaper. "We are just grateful that we found him. When he got home, he was delighted to get into his bed. We think he has realized how good his home comforts are now."

Perhaps Odi took the train to Ireland's capital because he heard that's where dogs were *Dublin* their fun.

NEAR AND DEER

A wacky deer made waves when he rushed into the ocean during a surfing competition and barely missed crashing into one of the dudes who was riding a crest.

At Salt Creek Beach in Dana Point in Orange County, California, the water was dotted with candidates looking to make the Dana Hills High School surf team during tryouts early one morning in 2016. Spectators who had lined the beach suddenly watched in disbelief as a male deer galloped past everyone on the sand and plunged into the water.

"We have no idea where he came from," Sheri Crummer, a judge for the tryouts, told the *Orange County Register*. "That was the craziest thing I've ever seen."

The deer was hopping over rocks that jutted out offshore and then he aimed straight for surfer Cody Foudy, who was having a great final run. As Cody was hanging ten, he came face-to-face with the deer. "Right away I knew it was a deer," the boy told Los Angeles TV station KABC. "It had giant antlers, and it looked right at my face. It was tripping me out because I didn't know what a deer was doing in the water." Cody was forced to kick his board away and bail out of the wave to prevent a collision.

But the buck didn't stop there. He began swimming out to sea. Wanting to rescue the wayward deer, Tim Samson, the surf team coach, grabbed his longboard. He paddled about a quarter mile out and managed to turn the deer back toward shore. It was a staggering sight. "Everyone was blown away," Crummer said. "No one had ever seen anything like this. Everyone was freaking out on the beach."

As the deer neared the beach, lifeguards kept spectators away from the water to give the animal a clear escape route. But the deer, perhaps thinking the waves were *just swell*, wanted to keep swimming. A boat from the Orange County Sheriff's Harbor Patrol motored close to the deer and, using a water hose, convinced the animal to get out of the ocean. When he emerged from the surf, the buck sprinted up the beach and disappeared onto the lush grounds of the Ritz-Carlton Hotel.

Orange County lifeguard captain Brad Herzog told the newspaper that it was rare for a deer to come down from the nearby canyons for an ocean swim. Added Crummer, "We thought the deer was just going in for a dip." Referring to an island 40 miles away, she noted, "But it looked like he wanted to swim to Catalina."

WHAT A KICK THAT WAS

Dusty the beagle came up with his own version of dodgeball—he was having a ball dodging professional soccer players whose game he interrupted for a full seven minutes.

The frisky dog was sitting in the stands with his human family, watching a British soccer match between Skelmersdale United and host Halesowen Town in West Midlands, England, in 2017. Midway through the first half, the crowd started laughing when Dusty scampered onto the field. The referee halted the game. But then the real action unfolded because Dusty had a goal in mind—not getting caught.

The players tried to nab the elusive beagle, with no luck. Laughing, the sportscaster for the televised match blurted, "This is the best highlight of the game so far." For the next couple of minutes, every attempt to capture Dusty failed, prompting the broadcaster to utter, "It can't be that hard to get a dog off the football pitch." Oh, yes it can, as Dusty proved. He kept weaving his way through the players as they lunged for him and came up with nothing but air. The crowd loved it, cheering every miss. "It's like no one wants the dog off the field," said the announcer.

Dusty was getting a kick out of his antics as he tested the defense—and patience—of the players. Running from one end of the field to the other, he showed off his skill of eluding everyone, including security guards. One player who tried, but failed, to coax the dog was Dusty's embarrassed owner, Asa Charlton, defender for Halesowen Town.

"I saw a dog come on, and I thought that cannot be my dog," Charlton told reporters. Oh, but it was. Once he realized it was Dusty, Charlton knew it was going to be a while before the chase would end.

"He had never been to one of my games before," the player said. "It was my mum's seventieth birthday, and she decided to bring him along with my wife and daughter, Lola. During the game, Lola was messing around with him, and he managed to slip off his collar and break free."

It took a minute or so before Charlton realized that the intruder was Dusty. The TV cameras showed the player placing his hands on his head in disbelief. "It was probably my worst nightmare," he said. "My wife, mother, and daughter were running about on the pitch of my match."

Several times after the fourth minute, players on opposite sides of the dog dived after him at the same time, only to have him squirm free from their grips. When Lola came out onto the field with a plate of food, Dusty stopped and gobbled it down. But sensing his pursuers were closing in, he bolted, leaving them face-planted in the turf, empty-handed.

The family then tried to tempt Dusty with a bacon treat. This time it worked. They grabbed him before he could flee. After putting on his collar, they led him off the pitch to a mix of cheers from those wanting to see soccer and those wishing the zaniness would continue.

In an understatement, Charlton said that Dusty was incredibly frisky—"and full of beans." At least the dog was a *keeper*.

BATHROOM BREAK

A bear broke into a house and used the living room as his own private bathroom.

Max Breiter, of Jackson Hole, Wyoming, woke up from a Saturday afternoon nap in 2017 when he heard his little dog, Rocky, barking furiously behind a closed door in another room. Breiter got the dog and planned to take him outside. While rubbing the sleep out of his eyes and carrying his pet, Breiter strolled into the living room, where he spotted a large animal in the open kitchen about 20 feet away.

"At first I thought it was a dog," Breiter told the *Jackson Hole News & Guide*, "but I started to wake up and realized it was a bear." Breiter was so shocked that he just stood there facing the equally shocked bear. Both stared at the other for about ten seconds before Breiter dashed off to the bathroom and locked the door behind him.

Using his cell phone, he called the seven other people who were in the house at the time. Rather than greet the uninvited guest, they locked themselves in their rooms and began yelling, in hopes that the noise would convince the bear he wasn't welcome.

Between their shouts and Rocky's barking, the bear got the hint, but not before leaving a calling card. "The bear walked into the living room and took two poops on the floor," Breiter said. "Then he broke out a screen window and proceeded to run down the hill."

Homeowner Sandy Hessler told the newspaper, "I'm not sure what to do because we have the windows open all the time. The whole idea that we could be sleeping and a bear walks in, well, I've never thought about it." Everyone in the house has thought about it since—and found it *unbearable*.

SKY-HIGH CAT

A stowaway cat got the ride of her nine lives—on the wing of an open-cockpit aircraft.

Minou, the black-and-white mascot of the ULM Flying Club in Kourou, French Guiana, liked to take naps in cozy spots throughout the airfield.

On this particular day in 2015, she chose the wing of a parked Skyranger, a two-seat ultralight plane with fabric-covered, tubular construction. When pilot Romain Jantot, 28, decided to take a woman friend up for a short ride, he did a preflight check and walked around the plane without noticing the snoozing cat.

Minutes later, the plane was at an altitude of about 1,000 feet and flying at more than 80 miles an hour. Jantot had turned on an onboard camera, which was aimed at him and his friend. The pilot had no reason to suspect there might be another passenger onboard.

As the video shows, Minou suddenly appears hanging on to one of the tubes that held the wing, which rested over the cockpit. She doesn't look happy. With her fur blowing in all directions, her eyes bulging in fear, she meows frantically while clutching a support bar. But because of the wind and noise from the propeller, Jantot and his friend don't see or hear the freaked-out cat clinging to the left wing.

After the plane climbs some more, the video shows Jantot looking over to his left and finally noticing the mewing *air apparent*. His eyes grow just as wide as the cat's.

"I was extremely surprised when I saw her," Jantot told ABC News. "I think my reaction on the video speaks for itself."

Afraid the cat would recognize him and jump into his lap mid-flight, he avoided eye contact, powered back the engine, and began a fast descent. As soon as the engine began to slow down, Jantot noticed Minou became somewhat calmer.

Jantot landed the plane as smoothly and quickly as possible. The pilot then got out of the cockpit and went over to Minou, who was still gripping the support bar. He gently picked her up and placed her on the ground. Recovering from her fright flight, she scampered over to the flying club's office, where she found comfort by cleaning out the food from her bowl. Assured that Minou had no interest in another airlift, Jantot and his friend took off again.

Right after Jantot posted the video of Minou's wing-walking on YouTube, he predicted, "She is going to be famous all over the world." He was right. The video has been seen by millions of viewers. On YouTube, he wrote, "The cat is doing well. She is still our mascot."

For Minou, it was a *mewment* she would never forget.

RASCALS

SHEEPISH DOG

Rocky the border collie was simply too enthusiastic about his job. The overeager pup rounded up a flock of sheep and led them right into his owner's house!

The seven-month-old pup was still learning how to guide the sheep on the farm of Andrew and Rosalyn Edwards of Devon, England. One day in 2017, Rocky thought he knew all there was to know about herding. Seeing that a normally closed gate was accidentally left open and that no one was within sight, the dog took it upon himself to do what he was being trained to do. Well, sort of.

He expertly gathered nine sheep. But then came

the part of the training that he didn't quite grasp. Rather than direct them out to pasture or to their pen, he proudly guided them to the one place that felt like home. That's because it was home—for the farm family. He led the sheep straight into the unlatched back door of the Edwards's house.

Rosalyn told the BBC that she was in the kitchen when she heard sheep bleating. To her, it sounded as though they were inside the house. But she knew that couldn't be true. Until it was. She could barely believe her eyes. It was *shear lunacy*.

"I turned around, and the sheep were just standing there," she said. "There were about nine of them. I took the children into another room and then tried to guide the sheep out."

She wanted the flock to make a *ewe turn* and leave. But they weren't in any hurry, and Rocky wasn't much help because he thought this was a *sheep thrill*. The animals took a little tour of the house before they were shoved out the front door, leaving behind a smelly mess.

"I thought it was funny at the time, but then there was quite a lot of wee, poo, and mud everywhere," said Rosalyn, who posted a video on Facebook of the sheep in her house. "It took me a little while to clean it all up.

"Rocky did look quite pleased with himself," she

added. "But he's going to need more training." At least the family has a homespun *yarn* to tell.

FAIR-WEATHER FRIENDS

Sometimes TV weather forecasts can go to the dogs—literally.

Take Ripple, for instance. The part-mastiff, part-shepherd appeared on Canadian weatherman Mike Sobel's live segment on Global News Morning Edmonton in 2014 as part of Sobel's weekly feature of showcasing animals available for adoption from the Edmonton Humane Society.

Sobel had been doing this bit for more than a decade, but he never had a canine guest quite like Ripple.

Holding the big, high-spirited dog on a leash, Sobel started his forecast by saying—quite accurately, as it turned out—"This is going to be a challenge. This is Ripple . . . and Ripple likes to play." To prove it, the dog began pulling on his leash. "He's only a year and a half. He just wants to play. Ripple, sit! Sit!" Ripple ignored the command.

Sobel launched into his forecast, pointing at the weather map while hanging on to the leash, which the dog was now chewing. The pooch then yanked on it, pulling the weatherman off-balance. "Ripple's not sitting, that's for sure." Sobel continued delivering the weather, when the dog gave another hard tug on the leash. "Are you having fun there?" Sobel asked him.

Yes, most definitely yes. Ripple showed his strength by dragging the weatherman nearly out of the camera shot. "Nooo!" Sobel shouted before bursting into laughter. Remaining the consummate professional, Sobel returned to his forecast while struggling to maintain his balance during the ongoing tug-of-war.

Trying to catch his breath and stifle his laughter, Sobel said, "It starts to warm up nicely as we get to the weekend . . ." Just then, Ripple chewed through the leash, causing Sobel to hold up the frayed end in disbelief and guffaw. "You're on your own," he told the dog. Ripple then jumped at Sobel, nearly knocking him over as the dog tried to grab the remains of the leash in the weatherman's hand. As Sobel turned to face the camera, Ripple jumped again, hitting him in the back just as he said, "We'll be back in a moment . . ."

No weather segment on the show had garnered more publicity than Ripple's. The video went viral and was featured on CNN, *Good Morning America*, and *Inside Edition*, as well as scores of TV and news websites throughout the world.

"I've probably been doing those segments for about fifteen years, and I can certainly say this was the most rambunctious dog that I've come across," Sobel told *Inside Edition.* "But the bottom line was . . . I wanted to get that dog adopted."

The Ripple effect created a tidal wave of interest in him. The Humane Society fielded dozens of calls from people wanting to take Ripple. He was eventually placed with a family who had a Great Dane and plenty of acreage for him to play.

That same year, a frisky one-year-old American bulldog named King couldn't wait to get TV screen time on "Pet of the Week" on NBC 6 in South Florida, a weekly feature at the end of the newscast. He was so eager that he made his debut a few minutes early—during the station's weather report.

Ryan Phillips was standing behind an anchor desk when King broke free from his handler and scampered over to Phillips, who stopped the forecast, looked down, and said, "Hi, King. How are you?" King bounded onto the desk to show just how thrilled he was to be there.

Startled, Phillips shouted, "Whoa!" Wagging his tail furiously, King tried to lick Phillips's face. While trying to hold back the lovable, wiggling dog, the weatherman said, "Live TV. How are you, buddy?" King kept squirming in his effort to plant kisses. Fending him off, Phillips said, "It's not your turn yet. You have to wait one more segment. Okay?" The studio crew roared with laughter. "Just let me do the weather," Phillips pleaded with King. "I know you're stoked. So are we."

Talking to the director, Phillips said, "Let's just go to the weather map so we can get him off of here in a graceful fashion." The camera cut away to a graphic while someone grabbed King. The next shot showed Phillips by the weather map. As he started the forecast, he said, "Is this going to be on YouTube later?" You betcha. As for King, well, days later he was blessed with a new *fur-ever home*.

HIGH TIMES

A young raccoon kept animal lovers the world over on the edge of their seats as they watched on social media her death-defying climb up the side of a 25-story skyscraper.

It's anybody's guess how many hours of work were lost or how many fingernails were chewed as people tracked her agonizingly slow ascent. She had them tied in emotional knots as they wondered if they would be witnessing her successful scale to the roof or her untimely demise.

At about 11 a.m. on June 12, 2018, the normally nocturnal animal was spotted curled up on a ledge of the two-story Town Square building in downtown St. Paul, Minnesota. Nobody knew how or why she ended up 20 feet above the street. Three maintenance workers put up a tall ladder, hoping she would use it to get off the ledge.

The raccoon was clearly not ready for any kind of *climb-it control*. She dug her long claws into the building's exterior and worked her way next door to the attached UBS Plaza. Then she started to go up the side of the pebbled-concrete-textured skyscraper. Within minutes, she was five stories high.

And that's when she began attracting a worldwide audience. Passersby looked up and gaped in horror, worried she would fall. Office workers in other buildings stopped what they were doing to watch and snap photos and videos of this uplifting event.

Minnesota Public Radio (MPR) reporter Tim Nelson tweeted constant updates of the high drama, using the hashtag #mprraccoon. When the raccoon had climbed to the twelfth floor, she was a mere blob between two windows more than 100 feet above the street. If fretting bystanders couldn't get a grip, she could. She ascended to the fifteenth floor and then up to the twentieth.

A marquee on MPR's building across the street flashed the breaking news: "St. Paul's downtown raccoon reaches new heights."

While climbing 20 or 30 feet up a tree is not unusual for a raccoon, scaling a skyscraper is, Russell L. Burke, a biology professor at Hofstra University, told the *New York Times*. "That kind of height is extraordinary," he said.

People around the world were following the raccoon's high adventure on Facebook, Twitter, Instagram, and other social media, as well as on television and radio. By night, the bandit-faced daredevil was the most talked-about story online, more popular than news of the historic meeting between President Donald Trump and North Korean leader Kim Jong Un.

Fortunately, the critter had friends in high places. Officials with St. Paul's Department of Safety and Inspections, which includes Animal Control, decided against breaking out a window or lowering window cleaners to capture the raccoon because they feared she would get scared and might panic and fall. They chose to leave her alone. But they had a plan to save her. They brought traps onto the roof and baited them with cat food, figuring the smell would lure her to climb the final two floors to safety.

Having spent several hours ascending the skyscraper, the high-maintenance varmint seemed exhausted and went to sleep on the ledge on the twenty-third floor. At about 10:30 p.m., she woke up. To the surprise of those who were keeping an eye on her, she began heading down. But she stopped on the seventeenth-floor ledge.

A photographer with a telescopic lens snapped a photo of the critter peering over the ledge. Probably thinking it was a long, long way down, she reversed course and started climbing up again around 2 a.m.

About 45 minutes later, she reached the top and jumped onto the roof. She went over to the tempting cat food and water inside the trap and wound up confined with no way to escape.

Later that morning, members of Wildlife Management Services, the company that set the traps, recovered the plucky climber. Laurie Brickley, a spokeswoman for the city's Department of Safety and Inspections, told reporters the raccoon was a two-year-old female. "She was a little skinny but in good shape," she added. The animal was "incredibly tired" and had consumed all the food and water that was in the trap.

Later, the company said on Facebook that the raccoon had been released on private residential property in the suburbs of the Twin Cities with permission from the owner, and after consultation with the Wildlife Rehabilitation Center of Minnesota.

"We were all impressed by its ability to keep climbing," St. Paul mayor Melvin Carter told MPR. "We were all nervous and scared. Glad we have a happy ending."

HOUDINI HOUND

Nothing was going to keep General, a clever ten-year-old Great Pyrenees, from escaping a boarding kennel—not one door, not two, not three, not even four doors.

In 2017, Travis Campbell and his family were going on a beach vacation, so they boarded their dog at the Aquia-Garrisonville Animal Hospital in their hometown of Stafford, Virginia.

"He is very special," Campbell told Washington, DC, TV station WGGT. "He is a smart dog." When the family dropped General off at the animal hospital, Campbell made a point of telling the staff, "Opening a door is nothing new for him." But with all the facility's doors and enclosures, it seemed impossible for General to slip out.

General behaved himself after being put in an enclosure that had a latched screen door. But all the while he was plotting his escape. "Basically, he spent a day and a half trying to figure out how to open the door from the inside," Campbell said.

Security video showed that around 2 a.m., General used his nose to unlatch the door of his enclosure. Then he pushed open the door. "It's a trick to lift the latch from the inside, and he figured it out," Campbell said. "Pretty impressive."

General got a little scratch on his nose, but that didn't stop him from opening the next door, a heavier wooden one. Using his teeth, he pulled down on the lever and, while still gripping the lever, backed up to swing open the door. Then he scrambled through before it closed. He did the same thing with another door that he encountered.

For the next two hours, he sniffed around the animal clinic. At about 4:15 a.m., he finally decided it was time to leave. He went to a side door and, with the same lever-gripping technique he had used with the previous two, opened the door and stepped outside. Hey, don't knock it. That's a remarkable trick that *hinged* on his intelligence.

Later that morning, the staff was shocked and mystified when they discovered General was missing. They found him 15 hours later, lounging on a neighbor's front lawn. Rather than board him, Campbell brought General to the beach so he could play with the family.

Referring to the famed stunt performer and escape artist, Campbell added, "General is a Houdini."

FOWL WORDS

Police detained a foulmouthed pet parrot because he swore at an elderly woman every time he saw her.

The victim, who went by the name Janabai, filed a complaint with the cops in the town of Rajura, Maharashtra, India, in 2015, claiming Hariyal the parrot and his owner made abusive and obscene remarks whenever she walked by their house. She further stated that her stepson, Suresh Sakharkar, owned the bird and had spent two years training Hariyal to spout insults and dirty words specifically at her.

Janabai and Sakharkar were estranged and locked in a bitter legal dispute over ownership and control of property.

"I have been harassed for the last two years," Janabai told Indian TV channel Zee News. "On seeing me, the parrot uses bad language and foul words. That is why I have complained thrice in the last two years. Police should investigate and seize the parrot."

To determine whether a crime had been committed, police summoned Janabai, Sakharkar, and Hariyal to the station. The cops wanted to hear Hariyal's nasty language for themselves.

Whether the parrot was trained before the meeting to stay mum or was smart enough to know that anything he said could be used against him, he kept his beak shut at the police station. He was a model bird, a silent bird, even when he saw Janabai. "We watched the parrot carefully, but he did not utter a word at the police station after being confronted by the complainant," Police Inspector P. S. Dongre told reporters. At least the cops didn't have to give the parrot a *polly-graph* exam.

After studying the issue, the police came up with a compromise. In exchange for not charging Sakharkar or Hariyal with verbal abuse, police turned custody of the bird over to officials of the Maharashtra's forestry department. That way, Janabai was spared any further harassment, and Hariyal was free to fly—and swear—to his heart's content. Then again, maybe he was just all *sworn out*.

PUTTING HER MONEY WHERE HER MOUTH IS

Holly the Labrador retriever is one money-hungry dog. In fact, she is obsessed with cash, so much so that she tries to steal dollar bills whenever she can. And it's no wonder. She uses them to buy treats.

"It started when she was a puppy," her owner, Casi Cook, told the Dodo. "She used to steal stuff out of our bags, including money, and instead of chasing her around the house, we would kind of bribe her with treats. When she had money in her mouth, we didn't want her to eat it, so we would say, 'Here, Holly, take the treat and give me the money.' It clicked in her head that if she has the money, she will get treats."

Because of this conditioning, and the fact that the black Lab is really smart, Holly knows the value of a dollar bill. A buck can buy her a doggy bone.

Holly, whose passion for greenbacks brought her worldwide attention in 2017 on television and social media, enjoys giving her human family a run for their money—literally. They've had to chase her around the house when she snatches cash.

"She is a money fiend and thief," Cook told *People* magazine. "If she steals a dollar from us, she will hide the money by putting one of her toys in front of it. There are dollars all over the house—in the kitchen, the living room, on the stairs, in the hallway, in my bed. Everywhere you turn, there is a dollar there."

Cook, a restaurant server, said that she has to be careful when she brings home tips from her job. "Holly even knows when we count money," she said. "She can hear the [counting of] money from a mile away. She's too smart for us.

"If you tell her 'Go get a dollar!' or 'I will give you a cookie for a dollar!' or 'Where's a dollar?' she will run around the house until she finds one." When the money that she has squirreled throughout the house is gone, the family restocks it in various rooms.

Sometimes, Holly won't wait to be asked if she wants a treat. She will initiate a deal. "When we are at the dinner table, she will quietly walk up to one of us and just gently place a dollar on our laps and look at us with that puppy face," Cook said. They always give in, and off she goes with her treat. For Holly, it's all about *cash and carry.*

FRAIDY-CAT

George the cat single-pawedly delayed more than 80 subways and thousands of riders for up to 40 minutes in Manhattan after he escaped from his owner and ran onto the wrong side of the tracks, where he lost his train of thought.

Mila Rusafova, 23, of Washington Heights, had taken George and another cat, Zoe, to the animal clinic for routine checkups in 2015. Shortly after 5 p.m., she and her pets were waiting at the Canal Street station for the uptown train to take them home. While Zoe was in a carrier, Rusafova kept George on a leash because she considered him a "super chill" cat.

But he turned into a scaredy-cat when the E train rumbled into the station. Spooked by the noise, he broke free from his collar and leaped onto the railbed. The frightened one-year-old black cat hid in an alcove cut into the side of the subway tunnel's wall across from the platform and dangerously close to the electrified third rail. Aligned just outside the tracks, the third rail carried 625 volts and provided power to the trains.

Rusafova was worried that if George ran off toward another spot, he would touch the third rail and get electrocuted. But for the moment, the cat was too freaked out to move and remained frozen in terror, his back to the subway.

Along with other riders on the platform, Rusafova flagged down an uptown E motorman as the train pulled into the station and begged the driver to get help for George. The Metropolitan Transportation Authority (MTA) soon shut off the power to the tracks. It suspended service on the E train route and delayed or rerouted other trains, inconveniencing thousands of passengers.

"Time was a blur," Rusafova told the newspaper *AM New York*. "That whole time, George never moved. He was frozen to the spot. I was always scared that he would run."

With the power off, transit officers Gus Vargas and Brian Kenny hopped in front of the E train at the station to rescue George. While Vargas made sure George wouldn't take off down the tracks, Kenny, an avid cat lover, slowly approached the shaking feline. "He was panting, he was petrified," Kenny told the newspaper. "He didn't move a muscle. The third rail was within four inches of his tail. I gave him a little scratch on the head. When I picked him up, he reached for both of my shoulders like a baby. He almost hugged me."

Kenny handed George to Rusafova as riders on the platform applauded. It was about 5:50 p.m. "It was one of my worst nightmares come true," she told *AM New York*. "I'm very grateful to the NYPD and with the MTA's patience."

Because of George, an estimated 10,000 commuters faced up to 40 minutes in delays during the evening rush hour. The MTA said that 83 trains on the A, B, C, D, E, and F lines were rerouted or delayed.

But at least George was rescued and was *feline fine*. Said Officer Kenny, "George used up a bunch of his nine lives."

VANDALS

WATER YOU DOING?

Baloo, a five-month-old fun-loving border collie, relished playing in water gushing out of the sprinkler on the front lawn. But one time in 2018, his frolicking caused him to end up in hot water.

When he was just a few months old, his owner, Cara Wohr, of Lake Dallas, Texas, introduced Baloo to her oscillating sprinkler, which moved back and forth while shooting out several streams of water in a big wave-like pattern. Every time the sprinkler was on, the dog couldn't resist jumping back and forth through the spray or, when tired, just standing over it and letting the water squirt his belly. There was no doubt that the sprinkler was his favorite toy, and his antics brought laughter to family, friends, and neighbors.

One summer day when the temperature soared to a scorching 106 degrees, Baloo, who was named after the bear in the children's classic *The Jungle Book*, was outside getting soaked by the sprinkler. This was when the puppy had a great idea: If he could be having this much fun outside on one of the hottest days of the year, imagine how much more fun he could have by playing with the sprinkler *inside* the house, where it was cooler.

Wohr told *People* magazine that she was reading in her bedroom when she heard a clanking sound, so she got up to investigate, and what she saw left her speechless. There was Baloo having the time of his life, playing with the still-running sprinkler—in the family room! He had dragged it through the doggy door and now, as he happily jumped from side to side, the sprinkler was drenching the tile floor, rug, table, lamp, television, and leather couch.

"I was in a panic on what to do," Wohr told *People*.

After collecting her thoughts but before turning off the water, Wohr took a few quick pictures on her cell phone to document her dog's shenanigans. She put one of the photos on Facebook. It shows Baloo leaping over the sprinkler as it spews water throughout the wet room.

Within days, it had more than 120,000 shares, including from people as far away as Germany.

Wohr mopped up the mess and was grateful that none of the furniture was ruined. Now she keeps close tabs on Baloo whenever she waters the yard. It's a *lawn distance* relationship.

GOATS ON THE LAM(B)

No *if*s, *and*s, or *butt*s about it, more than 100 goats unexpectedly raided a sleepy residential neighborhood in Boise, Idaho, early one morning in 2018. The hungry herd went from one lawn to the next, chewing grass, munching on plants and bushes, and stripping trees of low-hanging leaves.

Shortly before 7 a.m., 118 adult and baby goats appeared on Summerwind Drive in the west side of town and began eating their way down the street, to the surprise of early risers. The new kids on the block soon attracted a crowd as neighbors—some in their pajamas—rushed out of their houses to take photos and videos and pet the friendly goats. Not everyone was amused. Some shooed the invaders away before they destroyed flowerbeds and gardens.

Joe Parris was the first TV reporter to break the news live on KTVB's morning newscast. As the camera zoomed in on a group of goats gobbling up a rosebush, Parris said, "Right now they're having a morning snack. It's been going on for about an hour. The neighbors don't know where they came from. Animal control is here, and they initially showed up with one truck, and they realized rather quickly that wasn't going to be enough. For now, the goats are going from yard to yard eating everyone's front lawn. I talked to one neighbor who said, 'Well, at least I won't have to mow my lawn this morning.'"

Neighbor Ben Dunn later told Parris, "Half the neighborhood's lawns have been cut. I mean, mowing for free!"

The mystery of who owned the goats was solved about 90 minutes after the *goat-nado* began, when a truck from a local company called We Rent Goats showed up. According to its website, the firm loans out its goats "to remove noxious weeds from fields, acreage, pastures, open spaces, ditches, ravines, embankments . . . You name it, and the goats can clear it."

Kim Gabica, who owns the company with her husband, Matt, said the goats had been grazing along a nearby storm retention pond throughout the night. Shortly before sunrise, they made their escape. "They managed to break through a fence and go on a little adventure to meet the neighbors," she told Parris.

With the help of residents, the Gabicas rounded up all the goats and loaded them into a trailer. Before the animals were taken away, Kim told Parris, "They're very creative escape artists. Just when you think you have all the containment figured out, they find a way that you didn't think of." She added that the fence would need repairs before the goats could return to grazing at the retention pond.

By 8:30 a.m., the "goat-a-palooza," as Parris termed it, was over. But the social media Twitterstorm was just beginning. Some of the tweets:

"Who you gonna call? Goatbusters!"
"Well, there goats the neighborhood."
"Oh, no!! It's Arma-goat-in!!!!"
"This story really got my goat."

LEAVE IT TO BEAVER

A beaver with a Grinch-like attitude waddled into a store and started to knock Christmas decorations onto the floor.

It might have been the holiday season, but the wild animal obviously wasn't in the mood after he entered the Dollar General store in Charlotte Hall, Maryland, in December 2016. As shoppers gawked, the critter headed over to a display of small artificial trees and decorations. Then, showing he didn't care about the festive items, he started shoving them off the shelves.

Not knowing what to do about this vandal, a shocked store clerk called the St. Mary's County Sheriff's Office for help. Corporal David Yingling drove to the crime scene, bringing along a member of the county's animal control division.

When authorities arrived, they witnessed firsthand the beaver heaver's dislike for the Christmas decorations, which were strewn on the floor. Catching him red-pawed, the animal control officer apprehended the furry hooligan. The critter was then turned over to a wildlife rehab center and later released. Presumably, he wasn't sent up the river.

HOME ON THE RANGE

Pets left alone in the kitchen can be a recipe for disaster. They can end up doing a slow burn . . . of the house.

For example, two golden retrievers, whose names weren't released by authorities (apparently to save them from embarrassment), were home alone in Southwick, Massachusetts, one morning in 2018. Roaming free in the house, one of the dogs noticed that the owners had left several pancakes on a plate on top of the stove after breakfast.

A security camera in the house revealed what happened next: After sniffing the aroma of the still-warm flapjacks, the retriever walks over to the stove, gets on his hind legs, and snatches a hotcake off the plate. He trots over to his bed and scarfs it down. Then he goes back for a second pancake, only this time when he rests his front paws on the stove, he knocks the plate off. It crashes to the floor and shatters. Startled by the mishap, he backs away. But his paw hits a knob and accidentally turns on one of the stove's burners.

A container sitting atop that particular burner quickly catches fire. Smoke begins forming a cloud around the kitchen ceiling, triggering the alarm. The dog runs out of the room, then returns and hops onto the couch in the family room, which is open to the kitchen. From there, his buddy joins him and the two peer over the back of the couch and watch helplessly as the flames on the stove create more smoke.

The culprit drapes himself over the arm of the couch, with his head down, as if thinking, "Oh, what have I done?" A few minutes later, he stares at the burning stove with a look of, "I'm in big trouble now." Meanwhile, his companion remains on the couch, not wanting any part of this potential calamity.

Fortunately, the home was connected to a monitored alarm system that alerted emergency responders. As the video showed, smoke continues to swirl and grow darker near the ceiling, when two police officers break into the house. One of them runs over to the stove and turns off the burner and puts out the fire. The other officer pets one of the dogs as if to reassure him that everything would be all right. Firefighters arrive moments later.

Aside from smoke damage, the house was spared any major loss. The dogs were not injured, although they were shaken up. The fire and smoke no doubt had *given them the crepes*.

Eight-month-old Emmy the cat was so hungry that she wanted to fix herself a meal, which became too hot to handle.

Early one evening in 2017, the black cat was alone in her owner's house in Adelaide, Australia, when she hopped up onto the kitchen's ceramic cooktop, where two boxes of cereal were resting. During her jump, she turned on the burner, which was underneath the cereal boxes. They erupted in flames, so she flew off the cooktop and scampered into the family room, where she hid under a TV cabinet.

As the fire grew larger and the smoke built up, passersby called firefighters, who managed to put out the blaze before it could destroy the entire house. "They reckon if it had burned for another three minutes, the whole place would've gone up," owner Jordan Pana told the local media. "We're very lucky." Perhaps, but Emmy's fire caused an estimated $40,000 in damages.

Pana recalled that when it was safe to enter the house, he searched for his cat and found her still under the TV cabinet. Later, with news cameras rolling, Pana held the purring perp in his arms and said, "This little one here had decided that she was going to cook dinner, and she jumped up and turned on the stove. She's a bit of an attention seeker, and she probably deserves an Emmy for this little performance today."

When a news crew filmed the burned and gutted kitchen, Emmy jumped onto what was left of the cook-top and strolled along the ruined counter as if nothing had happened. Ironically, Emmy started the blaze on International Cat Day.

FOWL PLAY

For whatever reason, Percy the peacock hated a new Range Rover in his neighborhood, and repeatedly attacked it. If his goal was to scratch and gouge all sides of the luxury sports utility vehicle, he achieved it with flying colors.

Percy was abandoned on a farm in Saint Lawrence parish, Jersey, which is one of the Channel Islands in the English Channel. Most of the locals knew Percy, who managed to survive on his own with the help of many regular handouts by the residents. Some people weren't fond of the colorful bird. He sometimes would raise a ruckus or prevent horseback riders from using a certain trail.

Like most people, Steve Wallace, owner of a kitchen design and installation company, tolerated the peacock, but in 2017 he ran *afowl* of the bird. "My friend and I were restoring a black Ford Capri in front of my house, and I looked at it one day to find it covered in scratches," Wallace told the local newspaper, the *Bailiwick Express*. "I initially thought that my grandchildren had done it and blamed them, but had to apologize when I saw what the bird was doing."

Apparently seeing his own reflection in the paint, Percy mistook it for another peacock and attacked the car. Wallace shooed him away and didn't see him again for several weeks.

Perhaps Percy was waiting to sink his claws into something newer and shinier, like the new Range Rover that Wallace brought home for his wife, Karen. A week later, Wallace noticed bad scratches on the SUV, which was parked in front of the house.

He didn't need a police investigation to determine the identity of the vandal. Percy showed up and boldly attacked the car for several days in a row.

"I came outside on the porch, and the bird was jumping up and down on the vehicle," Wallace said. "He was putting his feathers out and scratching the car. He sees his reflection in the car and thinks it's another peacock, so he tries to fight it. He is causing a heck of a racket."

The peacock scratched the car with his beak and claws in different places, including the roof, the sides, and the rear. Even after the Range Rover was covered by a net and blankets, the peacock returned for another round of vandalism. "I was standing a few meters away, and I saw him walk around the car. Then he started tearing the net and the blanket and launched at the car again. He keeps coming back and causing more damage [obviously paying attention to *de-tail*]."

"He has absolutely decimated the car," Wallace told the newspaper at the time. "Every single panel on the car has been scratched—the doors, the bumpers. The peacock absolutely hates it." Damage totaled about $4,500.

Attempts by Wallace, neighbors, and members of the local animal shelter to catch the wily bird had failed. "It's nearly an impossible mission to capture him," he said. "I spent an hour chasing him through the woods but I've found out he's quite good at flying because his wings aren't clipped. Every time you get close, he just goes away. There were four of us trying to catch him at one time, but we couldn't capture him. He's a big old bird. To rub it in, he always comes back after a while."

Percy finally got the message and no longer attacked the car. Still, for what he had done, Percy was, quite naturally, proud as a peacock.

A PAIN IN THE GLASS

What do you call an angry goat? *Butter.*

That was certainly true for one such four-hooved delinquent who deliberately bashed the glass front doors of a company before fleeing the scene of the crime.

The general manager for Argonics, Inc., a small polyurethane manufacturer in Louisville, Colorado, was the first person to show up for work one morning in 2017. He was stunned to see that the building's front doors had been shattered. "His instant reaction is, 'We've been robbed,'" engineer Greg Cappaert told the Boulder newspaper, the *Daily Camera*. "So he called police right away, and they are taking pictures and everything, and then he goes and checks the video."

What the executive saw in the footage of the

security camera proved that the culprit was the mischievous leader of a gang of kids who were up to no good. Except none of them were human; they were goats. In the surveillance video, the young goats are loitering in front of the building. Then their leader, a black-and-white older goat, starts ramming the building's glass doors.

"For like twenty minutes, he banged on the front door," Cappaert said. "He was trying to beat up the whole building."

In the video, the vandal finally succeeds in shattering the glass of the front door. Somewhat startled by the destruction, he and his buddies take off. But moments later, the goat gang returns. It's clear the leader isn't interested in gaining entry because he could have just walked through the door that he had destroyed earlier. Instead, he proceeds to head-butt the other front door until he smashes the glass to smithereens. After doing a triumphant 360-degree turn, the culprit and the kids flee for good.

When the company's general manager talked to police about the vandalism, "they thought he said *ghosts* did it, and they thought he was a crazy person," Cappaert told the newspaper. "But then he said, 'No, it was *goats*. You can come watch the video.' Everybody had a good chuckle over it."

The suspect and the kids left behind plenty of evidence of their involvement—poop pellets all over the front sidewalk. It didn't take authorities long to figure out where the perps came from. They had escaped from a nearby farm, where the embarrassed owner agreed to pay for the damages.

"I don't know why the goat did it," Cappaert told Denver TV station KDVR. "That was just to be mean, I guess."

"He probably did it for fun," Susan Schoenian, a sheep and goat specialist at the University of Maryland, told *National Geographic* magazine. She said the ramming likely had nothing to do with the goat seeing his reflection. Explaining that goats are naturally curious and independent, she added, "Their hard horns, combined with their curiosity, gets them into mischief."

No *kidding*!

BEAR A GRUDGE

Bears went on a crime spree in Durango, Colorado, in 2017 by destroying the interior of cars after unintentionally getting locked inside. Here are some tales of vandalism caused by these *barbearians*:

Kourtney Anderson, 17, said she was asleep at about 1:30 a.m. when she heard a car honking outside. "At first, I thought it was just some crazy guy driving past honking," she told the *Durango Herald*. Kourtney peered outside and saw her mother's 2003 Honda Pilot with its lights on and windows fogged up. A closer look revealed what was causing the commotion. A bear had opened the door, climbed inside the vehicle, and then became trapped when the door closed behind it.

Hoping her mother, Kaylie Smith, who was in another bedroom, was awake but not wanting to disturb her, Kourtney began texting her: "Something is in the car and just woke me up, like crazy. The car honked so long. It's a bear!"

Kourtney said she was too scared to go outside, so she kept sending late-night text messages to her sleeping mother. For more than an hour, the bruin tried to get free and frantically tore apart the passenger door until it swung open and the vandal fled.

Kourtney then ventured outside to survey the damage. "OMG, Mom, OMG. I just checked it out," she texted. "The entire passenger-side door is completely torn up. You can't even shut the door. It's so bad, Mom, you're going to freak out."

The bear had ripped apart door panels, seat upholstery, and ceiling mesh and left scat in the back seat, Smith told the *Herald*. She said she had awakened at 5 a.m. and saw her daughter's late-night text messages.

Smith was perplexed why the bruin targeted her car, because it had been cleaned the previous week and there was no food inside.

Twelve days later, a bear—possibly the same one—broke into another Durango vehicle. At about 4:30 a.m., Sherri Haldorson went out onto the deck of her house after hearing the horn blaring from her 2003 Nissan Pathfinder. She couldn't see inside because the windows were too steamy, so she walked up to the SUV and shined a flashlight into the windows. "There was a huge bear in there shredding the interior of my car," she told the *Herald*.

Not knowing what to do, she called the La Plata County Sheriff's Office, which dispatched a deputy. He managed to free the bear, but by then the interior was a mess. "The car is no longer safe," Haldorson told the newspaper.

Even though the doors were closed on her SUV, they weren't locked, so the bear was able to open a door. Unfortunately for the bruin, it closed and the animal was trapped. Haldorson said the only edible items in her vehicle were mints and gum, but no other food.

Joe Lewandowski, spokesman for Colorado Parks and Wildlife, said even gum and mints are enough to lure a bear into trouble. "Bears can smell that through a car window," he said. He strongly suggested removing anything from a vehicle that could attract a bear. He added that residents should lock the car doors and roll up the windows. "We haven't met a bear yet that's able to figure out how to unlock a door that's locked," he said.

Three months later, another Durango bear took vandalism to a new level—by stealing an SUV, crashing it into a mailbox, and then trashing the interior.

At about 5 a.m., the bear broke into a Subaru by opening the unlocked door. The bruin released the parking brake, causing the vehicle to roll down an inclined driveway and across the street, where it ran over a mailbox and several utility boxes.

When the bear couldn't get out because the door was closed, the beast tore up the interior of the vehicle in a frantic effort to escape. The bruin pulled the steering wheel straight off the shaft, ripped the radio out of the dash, and finally busted out the back window and fled. The vandal-thief left behind a telltale clue in the back seat—bear poop.

All the commotion woke neighbor Ron Cornelius and his wife, who found the wrecked Subaru in their yard. In an interview with the *Herald*, Cornelius joked, "Usually, I don't get up at five o'clock unless there is a bear driving a car down the street."

BONEHEADS

TIRED BULL

No one knows how he did it, but a prized bull was found one morning sheepishly standing in his corral, wearing a giant tractor tire around his ample belly.

"We never ever in our wildest dreams expected that to happen," owner Todd Vogel told the *Des Moines Register.*

The 11-month-old purebred Hereford bull, named M.A.D. Confession, definitely seemed *tired* of the whole thing when Vogel, of Weeping Fox Ranch in Hartley, Iowa, discovered the predicament in 2017. The ranch had used several large tractor tires during the winter months to hold feed for its bulls, including Confession. But the tires were never meant as playthings.

"Bulls that age are like teenage boys," Vogel said. "They have endless energy, and they're not happy until they're rolling something on the ground."

When the Vogel family found Confession wearing the tire, they videoed him and posted it on social media with the caption: "Crazy things that happen with silly bulls." Because you don't see a bull wearing a tractor tire very often, the video went viral.

"New attire at the Weeping Fox Ranch for this Hereford bull," Vogel's wife, Kris, is heard saying at the start of the 19-second video. "Don't know how he did it, and I don't know how it's coming off."

In a way, it was a rather *tireless* effort. Vogel said they put a bull halter on Confession, tied him up, and then yanked off the tire. "It took a little bit of wiggling, but we got it off over his tail and over his butt end," Vogel said. "It really wasn't that big of a chore.

"Since he cooperated, it was probably a five-minute deal."

It's not clear if Confession learned anything, because he was playing with the same object the next day. Apparently, he wanted to *re-tire*.

STUCK UP

Dixie the cow was stumped by a *tree-mendous* problem—she lodged herself between two trees and couldn't move.

The Middleton (Idaho) Rural Fire Department received a call in 2018 that it had never, ever taken before: A pet cow was found wedged between two tall trees in rural Canyon County. This was a fire call that firefighters had to see for themselves.

Middleton Fire deputy chief Victor Islas told the *Idaho Statesman* that no one is sure how Dixie became stuck, but it likely happened while she was scratching herself against the trees.

Dixie's owners were alerted to the situation by their barking dogs, who led them to the trapped cow. With her calf nearby, all Dixie could do was moo. The owners tried pushing and shoving her, but nothing worked. That's when they called the fire department.

Because firefighters had never experienced this situation before—frankly, who ever had?—they decided to *cow-ordinate* with a couple of firefighters from nearby Sand Hollow Fire Protection District, who had dealt with cattle before.

Islas told the newspaper that initially he and his

men were going to try foam, but after consulting with Sand Hollow, they decided to use lithium grease instead. "We ended up greasing the sides of the cow," Islas said. "We got four of us in the front, two in the back, and kind of just pushed her back. Once we got her moving backward, she was able to move pretty easily."

He described Dixie as a "lovable cow" who was friendly to her rescuers throughout the hour-long ordeal. After they freed Dixie, the firefighters made sure no cow would try scratching herself there and get stuck, so they blocked the area with tree branches. Yep, that's right. They used *cattle logs*.

A POOPY DAY

Gidget, a two-year-old English mastiff, made a big stink when she jumped into raw sewage at a wastewater treatment plant and needed to be rescued by firefighters in hazmat suits.

It wasn't entirely her fault. Some of the blame went to her playmate, a seven-year-old coonhound named Buddy, who led her into the smelly mess in 2018.

Mandi Smith, of Pueblo West, Colorado, who owns both dogs, told the Associated Press, "We have a hound dog that likes to play escape artist with the front door. When he gets out, Gidget follows." On a Sunday night, Buddy secretly let himself out the back door, so Gidget tagged along. They didn't return that night.

Later the next morning, Buddy showed up wet, muddy, and smelling awful. However, Gidget was still missing, so the family began searching for her.

About an hour earlier and six miles away, Tony Campbell, an employee at the local wastewater treatment plant, heard frantic barks coming from one of the sewage treatment ponds. When he went to investigate, he found Gidget struggling to keep her head above the stinky muck in one of the ponds, while a fretting Buddy was pacing nearby. When Campbell rushed toward the dogs, Buddy took off, leaving Gidget to fend for herself.

Because Campbell couldn't reach Gidget, who was clinging to a concrete wall of an aeration pond, he called the Pueblo West Fire Department for help. After firefighters arrived, they suited up in protective gear and worked their way to the edge of the raw sewage pond. They managed to snare Gidget with a catchpole and then lowered a ladder for her.

"We coaxed and urged the dog to come over, and she came up the ladder kind of on her own," fire department division chief Brad Davidson told the Dodo. Once she was in arm's reach, the firefighters grabbed her and hauled her out of the wastewater.

They showered the smelly muck off Gidget with a fire hose and then turned her over to rescue workers from the Humane Society of the Pikes Peak Region. "She was really exhausted," Davidson said. "She just wanted to sit down and do nothing, basically. She stunk pretty bad, poor thing."

At the shelter, Gidget was given two decontamination baths, but she still stunk to high heaven. Workers contacted the family to come get their poopy pooch.

Smith, who also owns a bulldog, said it was a happy reunion. "Gidget is just ecstatic to be home," Smith told the Associated Press. "Out of all the dogs, she's the baby of the house."

Smith said she thinks that Buddy had jumped into the wastewater to take a swim, and Gidget followed suit. Buddy got out and eventually ran home, leaving his canine chum behind. "Gidget is like an eight-year-old kid," Smith said. "She's got that mentality—happy-go-lucky, 'I'm doing what you're doing.' 'If you're jumping, I'm jumping.'"

Back home, both escapees were smothered with love . . . and shampoo. "They have gotten many baths, but they still smell," Smith said. "The poor bulldog is keeping her distance."

GOING FOR A SPIN

You've probably heard the expression "hung out to dry." Well, it's happened to kittens who took snoozes in the family dryer and ended up twirling in a real-life nightmare.

For instance, Sugar Cookie, a 12-week-old Siberian, provided a scare for the family of Jennifer Liotino, of Mooresville, North Carolina, in 2018. The feline was watching Liotino take clothes out of the dryer and fold them. When Liotino was called away, Sugar Cookie figured the dryer was the *purrfect* place for a nap and hopped inside.

When Liotino returned to fold the rest of the clothes, she decided they could use a little fluffing to get out the wrinkles so she tossed them back in the dryer. Not noticing that Sugar Cookie was in the machine, Liotino closed the door, turned the dryer on a quick cycle, and left the laundry room to complete another chore.

A short while later, Liotino heard distressed meowing and realized they were coming from the dryer. She opened the door and pulled the bedraggled kitten out of the clothes. Sugar Cookie's coat was hot to the touch and her hair was sticking straight up.

Unsure what to do next, Liotino took Sugar Cookie

outside to cool off and then rushed her to Carolina Veterinary Specialists in nearby Huntersville. The vets put the kitten on an IV for dehydration and performed several tests, including blood work. Fortunately, the results came back normal, and she was sent home to recover from her traumatic ordeal.

Sugar Cookie's spin in the dryer and her treatment at the vet's earned her the title of January 2018's "Most Unusual Claim of the Month" by Nationwide, the nation's first and largest provider of pet health insurance.

Since then, Sugar Cookie has refused to go anywhere near that nasty dryer.

Phoenix, a seven-month-old kitten, knew exactly how Sugar Cookie felt because the same thing happened to him—only he was tumbling in a dryer for about 20 terrifying minutes.

In 2013, his owner, Elfie De Temple, 17, of Arundel, West Sussex, England, took bedding for the family dog out of the washer and tossed it into the dryer. While the girl's back was turned, Phoenix jumped into the appliance and snuggled in the damp bedding. Not realizing her black kitten was in the dryer, Elfie turned it on and walked away.

For the next 20 minutes, poor Phoenix was revolving

around and around in super-high temperatures. His whirling world didn't end until the timer turned off the machine. Elfie's mother, Deryn, then opened the door and was shocked when the kitten tumbled out. He was barely breathing, nearly unconscious, and extremely hot.

Her husband, Ron Cole, tried to lower Phoenix's body temperature with cold water. "We did that for a few minutes and then rushed him to the vet," Deryn told the *Daily Mail*. "He barely looked alive at all, we were all so scared."

At the animal clinic, Phoenix was treated for mild burns to most of his body. Blood tests revealed he had ten times the normal amount of potassium in his blood, a condition caused by his exposure to the extreme heat. "The vets were fantastic," Deryn said. After six days at the animal clinic, Phoenix—who was aptly named because he came back from near death—was allowed to go home.

"I feel terrible, and I'll never forgive myself," Elfie told the *Daily Mail*. "I think Phoenix has forgiven me, though. He gave me a cuddle last night."

The family doubted that Phoenix would attempt another dry run in the machine. Said Deryn, "He walked up to the dryer, meowed loudly at it, and then scampered off."

TRIP OF A LIFETIME

When a three-year-old feline named Kitty Bitty went missing for days, weeks, then months, his owners assumed the worst—that he was in cat heaven. Imagine their surprise five months after he disappeared when they learned he was alive and well in California, 2,400 miles away.

"Nobody can believe it," his owner Teresa Cameron, of Pooler, Georgia, told the *Atlanta Journal-Constitution* about her pet's odyssey. "You never know with a cat, but I didn't expect him to be in California."

Cameron said her small tabby vanished on the Fourth of July in 2017, possibly spooked by fireworks. It's believed Kitty Bitty made it to a Pepsi bottling facility about 10 miles away in Savannah. No one knows how long it took him to get there or how long he stayed. But at some point, he hitched a ride in a semi and went for the long haul. "We can only surmise he somehow jumped on the back of a truck or on a pallet," John Welsh, a spokesman for the Riverside County Department of Animal Services (RCDAS) told Los Angeles TV station KTLA. "Somewhere in that truck the cat went undetected for quite some time."

The truck made several stops along the way, but Kitty Bitty was content to sit tight in the trailer of the semi. Being cooped up with all that Pepsi, he probably wished he could drink some of it because it would have been *sodalicious*.

When the truck arrived at a Pepsi distribution center in Riverside, Kitty Bitty left the trailer but stuck around the facility. Eventually, in December, an employee captured the cat, who was extremely skinny and suffering from hunger and dehydration. But he made a fast recovery after receiving care at the RCDAS shelter.

Luckily, Kitty Bitty was wearing a blue collar with a rabies tag that had his owner's and veterinarian's contact information. A shelter worker phoned Cameron, who recalled, "I was like, 'Okay, where are you?' He said, 'Riverside, California.' I said, 'Excuse me?' I about flew out of my chair. I was like, 'Are you kidding me?'"

Because Christmas was only two weeks away, the shelter workers wanted to get him home before the holidays. According to Welsh, the employees pooled their money to pay for Kitty Bitty's flight home. The local ASPCA also contributed by paying the airfare for its relocation team member, Therese Holmes, to accompany the cat. Workers at the shelter used markers to write messages of love on the cat's kennel.

When Kitty Bitty returned home, he found two things had changed: He was no longer allowed to go outside, and he had a new roommate—a golden retriever.

HOLED UP

In two separate incidents, dogs found themselves in deep trouble. They ran into holes and couldn't get out.

Jack, a 10-year-old Great Pyrenees, was lounging on the grass outside his family home in Pleasant View, Tennessee, in 2018, when a squirrel had the audacity to walk across his lawn. Jack chased after the furry intruder, who then scurried into a culvert pipe underneath the driveway. Refusing to give up the pursuit, the large dog charged into the culvert. And that's where he made a major miscalculation. You see, the pipe was only 15 inches wide and Jack was 17 inches wide. When he finally realized he was too big, he had squeezed his way in until he was stuck.

When Jack didn't show up for his meal—he had never missed one before—his family went looking for him. They heard him whimpering in the culvert and discovered his dilemma. He was so deep in the pipe, there was no way they could get him out on their own, so they called the Pleasant View Volunteer Fire Department and Cheatham County Animal Control (CCAC).

While the fire department sprayed Jack with water to keep him cool, workers began digging out the culvert on the far end, using a backhoe up to the side of the driveway. Six men worked several hours on the rescue mission.

"We ended up having to remove a little bit more of the culvert top, and then we crawled inside the culvert and hauled [him] out," CCAC wrote on its Facebook page. "You could literally see the relief in his eyes. You could also hear the sighs of relief behind us from the family eagerly awaiting to see their little boy safe and sound."

Jack was examined at the scene and then taken to a nearby animal clinic, where the veterinarian gave the dog a clean bill of health.

"Tonight, Jack is sacked out in front of a fireplace with a bed that is just right in size, near the ones he loves and with those who love him just as dearly," CCAC wrote. "Next time, Jack, leave the squirrels alone."

Jack could have learned a lesson from Rubin, a schnauzer who chased after a cat and got stuck in a tortoise hole in 2017. The little dog was rescued after four hours of work by four different agencies.

Rubin's owner, Toby Passmore, also owned an African spurred tortoise named Scully. The giant 100-pound tortoise loved to dig deep, elaborate tunnels in the backyard of Passmore's home in Chandler, Arizona. One of the burrows extended six feet underground.

That was the one Rubin entered while chasing a cat, who was seeking safety inside the tunnel. The dog couldn't quite reach the cat. What he did reach was the end of the line. Unable to move in either direction, Rubin was stuck in the burrow.

Passmore told Phoenix TV station KNXV that when he and his wife couldn't find their dog, they went out to the backyard, where they heard faint barks coming from underground. In the past, Rubin had occasionally slipped into Scully's burrows but always managed to get out without any trouble. Not this time.

"I immediately, frantically tried to dig him out myself," said Passmore. But this particular tunnel was much deeper than all the others. Passmore, who feared Rubin might run out of oxygen if he remained down there for too much longer, called for help.

He received more than he had hoped—the Chandler Fire Department, the City of Chandler Utility Services Division, the Arizona Public Service Electric Company, and Southwest Gas. During the rescue operation, city workers and firefighters used shovels and a backhoe and even brought in a camera to peer down into the hole to check on the poor pooch. They had to remove the dirt carefully to keep the earth from collapsing on Rubin and the cat, who was also trapped, even farther inside the tunnel.

Finally, after four hours of excavating nearly a ton of dirt, they had created a hole wide enough for Passmore to go in headfirst. Grabbing Rubin by his back legs, Passmore pulled the dog out of the hole. Rubin, who was covered from head to toe in brown dirt, shook it off to reveal his black coat. Then he trotted off, no longer interested in catching the feline, who remained in the tunnel, still too rattled to move. Workers left the hole uncovered until the scaredy-cat emerged on its own, dirty but unharmed.

Passmore thanked all the workers for giving his dog a "second chance at life." The owner, who has kept Scully for ten years, said he hoped Rubin would think twice about going into a tortoise hole. "They're awesome animals," Passmore said. "It's just if you have a dog that'll go down into the chamber of death that your tortoise digs, it's not a good fit."

ROUGH RIDER

During a cold winter's night, Gumbo the cat thought he had found a nice, warm, quiet place to curl up for a nap. He was mistaken, because where he chose to get comfy was inside the hood of a minivan—a minivan that soon took him on a wild four-hour ride as he clung to the engine block for dear life.

The 10-year-old house cat had been in a carrier held by his owner, Raven Huang, of Brooklyn, New

York, who was taking him to the veterinarian for a checkup in 2017. Gumbo had other ideas and escaped. For nearly two weeks, Huang and a friend alerted local animal groups and went knocking on doors in the Manhattan Beach neighborhood, hoping someone had seen the missing feline. They put up posters and flyers and posted pictures of Gumbo on Facebook. But no one reported seeing the cat.

Meanwhile, Dana Esses, who lived a few blocks away, detected an awful smell—like cat urine—in her Honda Odyssey minivan while she and her family were driving 240 miles to a ski lodge. They also thought they heard meowing during the drive.

After arriving at the Great Escape Lodge & Water Park in Queensbury, New York, they popped the hood. Were they in for a surprise! Peeking out from deep under the hoses of the engine block was an orange tabby.

"It was a shock to say the least," the 39-year-old mother of six told the New York *Daily News*. "The cat found his way to a warm place. He wasn't wedged or anything. He peeked his little head out when my husband came over and then retreated. It was incredible. He didn't look injured at all."

The family alerted a hotel security guard, who contacted the Warren County SPCA.

"Our dispatcher was laughing at the security

person," SPCA director Jim Fitzgerald told the *Daily News*. "They went back and forth over whether this cat could have hitched a ride from New York City."

Fitzgerald went to the hotel, donned protective gloves, and pulled the cat out. "He was lethargic, but he fought me for a little bit," the director said. "He was really tucked in there."

Hoping to find the cat's owner, Fitzgerald snapped some photos and posted them on Facebook. The cat was brought to the local animal shelter, where he was given food and water and a checkup. He was in good condition considering he had just hitched a high-speed ride for four hours under the hood of a minivan.

The Facebook post eventually united Gumbo with Huang, who drove to Queensbury to claim him after the cat had been missing for 13 days.

Esses told the *Daily News* that her children were delighted that Gumbo was back with his owner. "They've always wanted a pet. I said, this is the closest you're getting." She added with a laugh, "I've since ordered a little bumper sticker that says, 'No Vacancy.'"

THUGS

UDDERLY RIDICULOUS

Stormy the cow enjoyed a *roamin'* holiday. Not once but twice the 1,100-pound Hereford broke free from a live nativity scene in Philadelphia, causing traffic headaches for motorists and the police.

Stormy had joined two sheep, Basil and Blossom, and two donkeys, Sally and Biddi, in a manger scene outside Old First Reformed United Church of Christ during the 2017 Christmas season. Using real animals in the crèche had been a tradition at the church since 1973. For Stormy, it was her first year as a *herdliner.* It would also be her last.

While the other animals were content to remain in

place, Stormy was in the *moooed* to escape when no one was around. Shortly after 2 a.m., she left the gated manger and made it all the way to the I-95 southbound ramp, when a startled motorist spotted the cow and called police. The cops weren't equipped with lassos, so they sent for the Animal Care and Control Team of Philadelphia to get her into a horse trailer and back to the church.

Church officials would have been wise to *beef up* security to keep Stormy in the manger, because a few hours later, she sneaked out again. This time she was found at around 6:30 a.m. in a parking garage a few blocks away from the church.

At 7:56 a.m., the Philadelphia Police Department tweeted, "If you're in the area of 4th and Market, beware of traffic delays. A cow is loose. Again. No, we can't believe we're tweeting this either."

John Owens, program assistant at the church, said that after Stormy was returned to the manger the first time, she might have learned how to open the gate and let herself out again. There wasn't going to be a third escape for Stormy. She was sent back to her 15-acre home, the Manatawna-Saul 4-H Club in Roxborough. "She was starting to cause too much of a ruckus for us," Owens said. Stormy's replacement was one of her offspring, Ginger, a heifer who was born in March of that year.

Once Stormy was secured, the police tweeted, "You know, you start your day saying, 'Well, being a cop is a tough job, but at least I won't have to catch a cow today.' But wouldn't you know it? You're wrangling a bovine. Then you say, 'Well, at least I'll never have to do that again . . .'"

WHAT A HAM

A pig that escaped from its owner found itself arrested and in the back of a cop car.

In 2015, the Shelby Township (Michigan) Police Department received a 911 call from a woman who said a pig was on the loose, and she didn't know what to do. She said she was doing yard work when the pig came barreling toward her and chased her to the front yard before the animal became distracted.

"Officers responded and were able to detain the pig and get him in the back seat of the patrol car," Deputy Chief Mark Coil told Detroit TV station WWJ. "Realistically, the pig didn't give us much trouble."

Maybe not in the arrest. But in custody, well, it was *pee-you*.

"Let's say the pig, either out of excitement or otherwise, felt the need to use the back seat of our patrol car as a bathroom," said Coil.

As officers pondered what to do with the porker, they received a call from its owner.

"The owner realized that his pig was missing and called and said, 'Hey, I think the pig you have might be mine,'" said Coil. "Because we don't have pigs running at large on a regular basis, we returned him."

Coil said the owner was so grateful the officers caught his pig, he "was kind enough to clean up after his pig's mess" in the patrol car. Poop and pee were everywhere—on the back seat and on the floor. The vehicle reeked. "I think the pig feels that he got the last laugh," Coil said.

On its Facebook page, the department posted a photo, which went viral, of the pig in the squad car looking out the back window with a big grin on its face. The caption read: "Now we know why the pig is smiling."

GIVEN THE BOOT

Kitty was lucky he didn't get charged with obstruction of justice when he harassed a police officer who was giving a driver a speeding ticket.

The tiny black feline frolicked freely on his owner Carl Bittner's farm near Taylor, Texas. One day in 2015, Kitty—Bittner never bothered to name him—spotted Police Officer Keith Urban (no, not the country superstar) pull over an SUV. As the cruiser's dash cam video shows, Kitty proceeds to hassle the officer unmercifully over the next five minutes.

Urban leans against the vehicle and talks to the driver, when Kitty bounds out of the weeds and paws at the cop's boots. Urban shoos him away with a gentle nudge of his foot. Kitty comes right back and weaves his way through Urban's legs while the officer begins writing the ticket. Acting as if he's trying to save the driver from a ticket, Kitty climbs the cop's left leg and jumps onto his left arm.

Urban tries to keep writing, so Kitty latches on to the cop's chest and then scampers up onto the back of his neck. The officer shakes his head a couple of times, but the kitten doesn't get the hint and stays put. Starting to lose some of his remarkable patience, the cop dutifully continues filling out the ticket and then literally bends over backward and lowers himself before scraping off the pesky nuisance.

But Kitty's *felines* aren't hurt by the brush-off. He comes back for more. After again threading his way through the officer's legs a couple of times, the cat climbs the cop's left leg and onto his right shoulder. Then the cat hops onto the top of Urban's head.

Next, Kitty returns to the cop's right shoulder and peers down at the ticket. Apparently not liking what he sees, the cat jumps onto the officer's right hand to prevent him from completing the ticket. Urban is getting fed up with the harassment and softly pushes the cat to the ground.

Kitty won't be deterred. He tries to scale Urban's left leg again, but with a slow flick of his leg, the cop sends the cat back into the weeds. Once more, Kitty returns—but too late to save the driver. Urban has given him the ticket. The cat tries to pester the cop again, but Urban shoves him aside with his foot. The video ends with Kitty running after the officer as he walks to his cruiser.

Naturally, the video went viral. Urban told the *Taylor Press* he didn't get scratched or feel any pain because the cat didn't dig in with his claws. But it was a little embarrassing. "I think the driver of that vehicle was laughing," Urban said. "He even offered to get out of the vehicle and remove the cat." But he never got the *oppurrtunity*.

DOE WOE

A deer mugged an innocent man and made a clean getaway.

The hit-and-run, which was recorded on security camera, happened seconds after Cary McCook was dropped off by coworkers in front of the Stork's Nest

Inn in Smithers, British Columbia, Canada, one evening in 2017.

"I thought I was going to have a quiet, relaxing night," he told *As It Happens*, the popular radio show of the CBC (Canadian Broadcasting Corporation). "Turns out that fate, or I would call it nature, had other plans."

McCook, an environmental management representative at the Kwadacha First Nation in Fort Ware, British Columbia, had hopped out of a truck, said goodbye, and shut the door. He had taken three steps toward the entrance to the hotel when, he recalled, "I hear three gallops to my left before I could process that there was a deer. I tried to get out of the way, but my left leg wanted to go left and my right leg wanted to go right, leaving me standing in the middle.

"By the time I realized a deer was heading straight toward me, she was in full sprint and I was already in her way. She tried to jump over me. I'm only five feet, six inches tall. But she couldn't make the clearance and then, bam, I got hit by Bambi."

The flying doe slammed right into his chest and laid him out. The doe didn't stop to admire her perfectly executed tackle. "When I got hit, I went down," he said. "I looked up and she kept running." Fortunately, neither she nor McCook was hurt.

McCook got to his feet and tried to catch his breath.

"By this time, the adrenaline was pumping, and I was more in shock over what had just happened," he said. "I went to the truck and I asked my coworkers, 'Did you see that deer?' They said, 'Yeah.' And I said, 'That deer hit me.' And then we paused a minute to process it because we couldn't believe it. After that, we just had a big laugh about it."

When McCook entered his hotel room, he called family members to tell them about the assault. But no one believed him at first because his timing was bad. "Mind you, this is April first, so everyone's thinking this is an April Fools' Day joke," he told the radio show. "I called my mom and said, 'Mom, I got hit by a deer.' She didn't believe it. She said, 'Oh, right, Cary, good one.' And I'm like, 'No, I'm serious. I got hit by a deer in front of my hotel.' She still wouldn't believe me. So then I talked to my brothers, and they wouldn't believe me either. And I was laughing because it was so ridiculous."

After hanging up, he took a photo of the deer hair that was still stuck to his left arm from the impact and posted it to his Facebook page. "Still no one believed me," he said. "So I was lying in my hotel room that night and I thought, 'Hey, maybe there's a security camera pointing toward the entrance.' So I got up and checked, and sure enough there was."

The next morning, McCook and the hotel manager reviewed the video. "Lo and behold, we had camera footage of the deer running into me," he said. That's when he noticed why the deer was sprinting. The video showed that she was being chased by a small dog who veered from view when the deer barreled into McCook.

"The manager and I sat there and laughed," he said. "Then she said, 'You should show this to your friends and share it with the world.' I threw the footage on Facebook. And this thing just went viral. Everyone was sharing it. And my family said, 'Holy Day! You weren't joking! You actually got hit by a deer!'"

Getting jumped by a deer made McCook the butt of good-natured jokes from friends and family. "I was called the deer whisperer and Dances with Deer," he said. "It's awesome because laughter is good medicine, good for the soul. I'm okay and the deer is okay, so it's all good."

DOG COLLAR

Finn, a Jack Russell terrier mix, ended up in the doghouse after he was "arrested" and detained in the back of a police car.

His crime was one that was near and *deer* to him. He simply can't stand bucks, does, and fawns, and loves nothing better than to run after any that he sees.

Reid Thompson and his girlfriend were walking on a trail in the woods with Finn, in Kenora, Ontario, Canada, one day in 2018, when they let him off his leash. Normally, Finn didn't stray, but when he caught sight of a deer, the dog took off after it and disappeared through the brush, Thompson told the CBC. Finn ignored Thompson's shouts and whistles to come back.

About 30 minutes later, Thompson received a call from the Ontario Provincial Police (OPP) saying they had "detained" the dog, who was now in custody in the back of a police cruiser. The cops said that Finn had caused "some chaos" because it was running after a deer. The chase went along a road, across the grounds of a hospital, and then back onto the road, where an animal lover called police for help. Thompson said Finn and the deer "had a bit of a scuffle" and then they jumped over a guardrail and ran across the frozen Lake of the Woods. Eventually, the deer escaped unscathed, and Finn gave up the chase.

"The deer got away when the cop was chasing after Finn," Thompson said. "He's a pretty small dog, so the deer could've easily taken him."

The police collared Finn. But rather than lock him up, they decided to release him to his owner. When Thompson met up with the police, there was Finn staring out from behind the barred back window of the squad car, looking quite guilty. The sight of that hang-dog expression was too good to be left to memory, so Thompson snapped a photo of the little culprit's *arrested development*. Thompson's daughter Emme then tweeted the picture and it soon went viral. "He's a good boy," she said. "He just hates deer."

A Kenora OPP spokeswoman told CBC News that Finn and his owners were given a "stern warning" about staying on his leash, but otherwise the matter was dropped.

Thompson told Fox News that besides being a little sore from the chase, Finn seemed "pretty proud of himself, though he wasn't too happy about the bath he got afterward. The baby powder spritz spray didn't match the new bad-boy image he is trying to cultivate."

(E)SCAPE GOATS

Pet goats have locked horns with the police and wound up under arrest.

For instance, in Cherokee, Oklahoma, Whitey the goat, who goes by the alias Kevin, began tangling with the law in 2018.

"He's just a normal goat who eats a lot and does what goats do," his owner, Doug Murrow, told Oklahoma City TV station KFOR. But normal goats don't hang out at bars and get arrested by the cops.

Whitey began sneaking out of his fenced-in home and causing a stir in town, where he gained the street name Kevin. "We started getting animal complaints about him running loose and somewhere along the way, we tagged him with the name Kevin," said Ryan McNeil, chief of the Cherokee Police Department.

He said the cops fielded more than a dozen calls about Kevin's antics, including several alerts that the goat had entered a tavern even though he was underage. "Now when people call and see him out, it's not 'There's a goat loose.' It's, 'Hey, Kevin the goat is running loose again,'" said McNeil.

Every time Kevin escapes from his owner, an all-points bulletin goes out over the police scanners and ends up getting mentioned in the town's weekly paper, the *Cherokee Republican & Messenger.* "Kevin has been a regular for quite some time in the paper and quite a humorous read," said resident Tammy Harmon, a big fan of the goat. "One week, it's, 'Kevin, the wayward goat, is at 3rd and Kansas.' Or 'Concerned citizen reports he is at the bar. Transported by local chief back home and placed on house arrest.' It just doesn't get more humorous than that."

Harmon and fellow resident Curtis Robinson became so fond of the mischievous billy goat that they started a Facebook page for him. Within a couple of weeks, more than 800 people were following Kevin's adventures.

"Kevin and the police officer had a standoff on Grand and the highway," Robinson recalled. "Kevin refused to surrender at first, but he finally gave himself up and was apprehended."

The first night Kevin went to the bar, Chief McNeil called Murrow, the goat's owner, and told him cops had collared the goat. "Kevin had been down to the bar. I loaded him up and took him back home," the chief said. "He was put under house arrest [which means] you stick him back in his fenced-in area and hook the chain back on."

Kevin's run-ins with the law were short-lived after Murrow brought in a girl goat to prevent him from wandering. "She's keeping him from his wild side," Murrow explained. "He wants to stay home more."

Three years earlier, Goliath the goat acted like a spoiled kid and refused to leave a coffee shop, so he was arrested by the Royal Canadian Mounted Police.

In an official statement, the RCMP said that around 4 a.m., a goat strolled into a Tim Hortons restaurant in Martensville, Saskatchewan. Employees politely asked the goat to leave because he wasn't going to buy anything, and they weren't going to serve him. They walked him outside. But the rebellious goat turned right around and marched back through the restaurant's automatic doors. He did this several times. That's when employees called the Mounties.

When officers arrived, they tried to convince the goat to move on. But Goliath didn't want to obey the law. The Mounties then "arrested" Goliath and escorted him to their vehicle. They later said that the culprit was "very unhappy" with their treatment of him after they shoved him into the back of their vehicle.

The officers decided to take him home instead of a holding cell at their headquarters, said the RCMP statement. But that proved to be problematic because they didn't know who owned Goliath. At the time, they didn't know his name either. They knocked on the doors of several area farmhouses, but no one recognized the goat. So the officers took Goliath to a local animal hospital for safekeeping until they could locate his owner.

Later that morning, the Mounties announced, "We are happy to report that the goat is safe and sound, back with his owners after his adventurous night out on the town."

It turns out that Goliath had escaped from the care of the University of Saskatchewan Student Rodeo team, which had borrowed him from Lakeland College. Goliath was one of three goats from the college that had been used in a goat-tying contest at a rodeo in Saskatoon. He had chewed through his ropes and somehow managed to travel 12 miles to the Tim Hortons in Martensville.

Katie Dutchak, the student rodeo organizer, said Goliath was happy to be reunited with his fellow goats, Sparkles and Billy. After this adventure, Goliath realized he had to act his age because he's not a *kid* anymore.

CHOWHOUNDS

THAT TAKES THE CAKE!

Bella the black Labrador retriever picked the absolute worst time to devour much of a wedding cake—on the bride and groom's big day.

Scott Willis, 28, and Jackie Walker, 31, of East Boldon, South Tyneside, England, were set to tie the knot in 2017. The night before, Scott's sister, Donna McMahon, and her husband, Liam, of nearby Stanley, took possession of the three-tier wedding cake that a friend had lovingly crafted. Donna, who was a bridesmaid, promised to look after the beautiful creation and bring it to the reception on the wedding day.

The cake, made with a creamy white frosting, was

adorned with icing of roses and flowers. It was kept in a box, which was placed on a stand on the kitchen table. Even though Bella, the McMahons' dog, had a raging sweet tooth, Donna had no worries that their normally well-behaved pet would try to eat it during the night because Bella slept in a kennel in the kitchen.

On the morning of the wedding, Liam and Donna went into the kitchen to a shocking sight. There was Bella, with crumbs and icing clinging to her whiskers, sitting guilt-ridden next to a ravaged wedding cake.

"I screamed and burst into sobs," Donna told the newspaper the *Sun*. "The cake was totally destroyed, and Bella was sitting there looking at the ground knowing very well that she was in big, big trouble.

"But Liam was just as much to blame as Bella. The last thing I said to him the night before was to make sure he closed the door of the cage where Bella's bed is. Of all the nights to forget, he chose that one. Bella must have thought all her birthdays had come at once."

For the dog, sweet dreams had come to life.

Liam told the BBC that Bella's drooping ears and hangdog look read GUILTY. "She knew she had done wrong," he said. Even though Donna was extremely upset, Liam took a few photos of their shamefaced pet sitting by the partially eaten cake.

When Donna's sister Gemma, who was also a

bridesmaid, came over to the house, she knew something was wrong. "Donna met me at her front gate and was so pale and shaky that I thought for a second the wedding had been called off," Gemma told the *Sun*. "She showed me into the kitchen, and we were suddenly both standing there screaming.

"We were panic-stricken about what we would tell Jackie. We decided the best thing was not to tell her at all and hope we could somehow replace it in time. So we just told her that Liam would be bringing it to the reception."

Gemma and Donna frantically phoned every bakery in the area and posted messages on Facebook pleading for help. Dessert Heaven, of Stanley, came through and baked a wedding cake in under three hours.

Liam, a mortgage advisor, admitted he should have known better, considering how much Bella loved sweets. He told the *Sun*, "In the two years we've had Bella, I've only forgotten to close her cage one other time—and that night she ate twenty freshly baked cupcakes that were cooling in the kitchen."

He picked up the new cake—which cost about $100 more than the original one—and brought it to the reception in time. "I told every guest the whole story, and they found it funny," he told the BBC. "Scott and Jackie were the last people to find out." When the newlyweds learned about Bella's cake break, they howled with laughter, he said.

"Ironically, they forgot to hand out the cake after cutting it at the reception, so the only one who actually got any wedding cake that day was Bella."

BOO-HOO CHEW

Bailey the cocker spaniel bit off more than he could chew—but it was enough to cancel a long-anticipated dream vacation for her human family of five. You see, Bailey ate the passports of the three children.

Russell Mack, 35, and his partner Ella Arundell, 32, of Winchester, England, had made reservations for a weeklong vacation to sunny Majorca, a Spanish island in the Mediterranean Sea, with their children, Erin, 9, Tilly, 6, and Harry, 2. The family planned to join friends at an all-inclusive resort. To make the vacation more special, they were going to celebrate both Erin's and Harry's birthdays, so the hotel offered to bake a special cake and throw a party for the kids.

The only family member not going on the trip was Bailey. Apparently, that didn't sit too well with him.

A few nights before their planned departure, Arundell, trying to be super organized, checked in with the resort online. It was one less thing to deal with. Or so she thought. She left the children's passports on a side table and went to bed.

The next morning, Mack discovered Bailey had eaten and shredded chunks of the kids' passports. "Russell came upstairs and said, 'We're not going on holiday,'" Arundell told the *Daily Mail*. "He showed me the passports. They were all chewed up. I was devastated."

The couple spent the next two days desperately trying to save their vacation. They even tried to tape the torn passport pages and took them to Bournemouth Airport to see if authorities would accept them. Nope. "The passports looked like rubbish, but we were clutching at straws," she recalled.

Because the passports belonged to children, the couple couldn't get replacements through a one-day fast-track process that was available to adults. "For children under the age of sixteen, there are child protection issues, so it takes seven working days," she explained.

They had no choice but to cancel their $3,200 vacation, which they had paid in advance. Even though they had travel insurance, the company denied their claim because the cancellation had nothing to do with illness or death. It had all to do with Bailey's appetite for passports—something no insurer would think to cover. "It was so stressful and deflating," Arundell said.

Eventually, the children's passports were replaced.

After paying the resort an additional $1,300 as a change fee, they finally jetted a month later to Majorca for their vacation—a vacation without a certain cocker spaniel.

JUGHEAD

There was a reason why a one-year-old pit bull terrier mix was given the name Pickle—because he was in one.

Residents in the Meadowbrook neighborhood in Fort Worth, Texas, had seen the stray dog scrounging around for food in 2017. They ignored him until after the canine found a large, clear plastic jar that had once contained cheese balls. Trying to lick up every last crumb, he stuck his head in the jar, but then, *oh, cheese whiz*, he couldn't get it out.

For the next four days, he stumbled around the neighborhood. Several concerned residents, including Staci Szybowicz and her husband, tried to rescue him, but he eluded them. "He was very fast and didn't want anyone to get near him," she told TV station WFAA. Szybowicz posted an alert on a neighborhood website. Meanwhile, another resident contacted Fort Worth Animal Shelter workers for help.

"When they called us, they said the dog was actually laying down at this point," animal control officer Randal Mize told TV station DFW. Mize and a fellow officer went over to the dog and pinned him down. "Eventually, we got the [plastic container] off his head," Mize said. "And then the fresh oxygen almost caused the dog to pass out. It was pretty intense."

Mize said the dog was in bad physical shape, looking bony and ragged, and definitely in need of some tender loving care. "He was pretty dehydrated, so we brought him back to the medical treatment ward," Mize said.

Because the original call reported that the dog's head was in a pickle jar and that he was in a terrible predicament, animal control workers named him Pickle. After several days at the shelter, Pickle had sufficiently recovered and was sent to a foster family, who helped rehabilitate and socialize him so he could be adopted.

On its Facebook page, the animal shelter thanked concerned citizens who had contacted authorities, saying "this sweet boy [was given] a second chance."

GOBBLING GOOBER

Bubba the dog enjoyed a Christmas Eve feast that left her as stuffed as a turkey—because she ate almost a whole one meant for her owners.

The five-year-old Chi Apso—a teddy-bear-looking cross between a Chihuahua and a Lhasa Apso—was home alone for a short time while David Barrett, of

Prestwick, Ayrshire, England, and two other family members stepped outside in 2016. For their holiday dinner, Barrett's mother had cooked a large turkey breast, covered it in tinfoil, put a dish towel over it, and placed it on the kitchen table. She had also made all the fixings and kept those under wraps, too.

Barrett told the *Daily Telegraph* he wasn't worried about Bubba sinking her teeth into the turkey because she was an obedient pet who had never shown any tendencies to jump up on the table. Besides, they were going to be gone for just a short period. What they hadn't counted on was the effect the tantalizing aroma of a freshly roasted turkey had on Bubba. She just couldn't resist.

The little dog climbed onto the table and began gnawing on the turkey. With every bite, she wanted more, and in her desire to eat as much and as fast as she could, she knocked the turkey onto the floor, where she gobbled it down until there was hardly anything left. She stopped only when she collapsed from a serious case of overeating.

When Barrett came home, he found Bubba passed out on the floor, her stomach bloated to twice its size. Only a tiny scrap of turkey breast remained, its meat carved with teeth marks.

To his credit, Barrett didn't panic. Instead, he took a photo of Bubba while she was still lying on her side, revealing her swollen belly. He posted the picture on Twitter and tweeted, "No chance has my dog just scranned [eaten] the whole turkey? There's the culprit. She can't move."

Waking up from her food coma, Bubba made a fast recovery and didn't seem to suffer any lasting ill effects. All was forgiven, likely because Barrett's aunt had cooked two turkeys and was able to deliver a replacement to the family to save Christmas dinner. As for Bubba, well, she was being put on a strict new diet. She had to quit *cold turkey*.

EIGHT IS ENOUGH

It's a crime what some animals eat. Seriously, it's a crime. At least it was for eight donkeys who ended up in jail for consuming something that wasn't theirs.

In the small town of Orai in Uttar Pradesh state in northern India, officials had planted nearly $1,000 worth of greenery near the local jail as part of a campaign to beautify the area. The residents applauded the new landscaping.

But they weren't the only ones who found the expensive saplings appealing. So did eight donkeys belonging to a young man identified only as Kamlesh. When he failed to pen them in one day in 2017, they strolled into the center of town and lunched on the young trees right down to the roots. It turned into a costly meal.

When officials discovered what the donkeys had consumed, they were outraged. Obviously, the animals couldn't pay for their meal with rupees, the Indian currency. No, they would have to pay for their crime with jail time. So the "h8ful eight" were rounded up and herded straight into the slammer. And not just for the night. Nope, they were locked up for four days with no chance of *bale*.

Kamlesh, the donkeys' owner, didn't know at first what had happened to his animals, according to the *Times of India*. When he found out they were behind bars, he pleaded with police officers to release them. The cops refused. In desperation, he persuaded a local politician who carried some clout to accompany him to jail. This time, the police agreed to release the culprits, but only after Kamlesh signed a promise that "from now on he will not allow his animals to roam in residential areas or places of public importance," according to an official statement.

TV cameras were there when the donkeys emerged from the seedy-looking jail and walked single file down the street with their heads bowed, like a classic police perp walk.

News of the arrest spread throughout India and

drew plenty of ridicule. "Dear UP Police," one person tweeted, using the abbreviation for Uttar Pradesh. "How about arresting real criminals instead of donkeys?"

BINKY BANDIT

Dovey, a wrinkle-faced Shar-Pei, caused some new wrinkles on the face of his owners because of his penchant for eating pacifiers—nearly two dozen of them.

The three-year-old dog had never caused any problems for his human family. When the couple had their second child in 2017, he was *lovey-Dovey* with the baby. One of the reasons, the owners would soon discover, was that the dog had a hankering for the infant's binkies, or pacifiers.

"Because of the baby, we had binkies throughout the house," owner Scott Rogers, of Edmond, Oklahoma, told TV station KFOR. "Over the previous months, we noticed binkies were missing, and we thought we left them in restaurants or they fell in couches and were lost."

No one suspected that Dovey was eating the pacifiers. "She had been drinking and eating and playing and running and acting normal," Rogers said. But then she began coughing up phlegm regularly and losing weight.

Only when the baby's grandmother caught Dovey

snatching a pacifier off the kitchen counter did the family suspect that their dog was sick from eating binkies.

Rogers took her to the Gentle Care Animal Hospital, where she was X-rayed. Their hunches were confirmed. Reading the X-rays, veterinarian Chris Rispoli counted seven binkies in Dovey's stomach. Because they were too big to pass through her intestines, surgery was the only way to get them out.

During the operation, the vet didn't remove just the seven that appeared on the X-ray. Nope, he extracted an additional 14, for a total of 21 pacifiers. "They just kept coming out," the vet told KFOR. "This was the most fascinating and exciting surgery I have ever done."

The operation went smoothly, and so did Dovey's recovery. She might not have learned her lesson, but her owners sure did. They have since kept track of every binky in the home. Hopefully, that will *pacify* any of their worries.

GRIN AND (TEDDY) BEAR IT

Maisy the St. Bernard enjoyed playing with other dogs' teddy bears and plush toy animals so much that she stole them and then ate them.

No one would have known if she hadn't become sick of committing her crimes.

The eight-year-old dog often took teddy bears that belonged to the family's other pets, two Chihuahuas, and gnawed on them and shook them. But she had never shown any desire to eat the plush toys.

In 2018, the happy-go-lucky gentle giant was no longer acting so happy. Something was clearly wrong. Her owner, Jane Dickinson, of Roberttown, West Yorkshire, England, took Maisy to the Paragon Veterinary Referrals. A CT scan seemed to show that she had a possible tumor in her stomach and a mass on her spleen. The diagnosis was grim: potentially terminal cancer. Surgery was the only course of action.

When veterinarian Nick Blackburn opened up the dog's stomach, he discovered that she wasn't suffering from any cancer. She was suffering from consuming her canine buddies' plush toys—four of them, to be exact.

"It's fair to say this was not something we were expecting to find," Dr. Blackburn told the *Daily Express*. "We all know certain dogs enjoy chewing things they shouldn't, but managing to devour four full teddy bears is quite a feat. We were naturally delighted the operation was such a success, and we were able to return a happy, healthy dog to the Dickinsons."

The family was overjoyed but also perplexed by her appetite for teddy bears. "The toys weren't even hers," Dickinson told the newspaper. "She would steal the

Chihuahuas' toys and play with them, but I've never seen her trying to chew them." Of course, that would explain how the teddy bears disappeared.

When the doctor showed Dickinson the four teddy bears, she didn't recognize one of them. But that mystery was soon solved. "My brother also keeps Chihuahuas," she said. "It turns out that one of the teddy bears belonged to his dog."

TROUSER BOWSER

Myles the Great Dane wears a coat and pants.

You're probably visualizing a dog in a trench coat and trousers. Don't. Actually, his short hair gives him a shiny coat, and he pants through his mouth like all dogs do. But unlike other dogs, Myles *eats* pants.

That weird appetite earned him recognition in Nationwide pet insurance's wackiest claim of the month for March 2016.

The one-year-old 150-pound goofball lived in Poughkeepsie, New York, with his owners, Matthew and Cassandra Orser, and their daughters Norah and Emma. The couple began noticing that small articles of their daughters' clothing were disappearing. They soon found out why when Cassandra caught Myles running to his crate with one of the girl's socks in his mouth.

"We figured out his routine," Cassandra told Nationwide Insurance. "He would steal clothes and run to his puppy crate to eat them. We were finding pieces of socks and fabric in his [poop] out back. Even though he weighs more than 100 pounds, he's still a puppy and his training is still a work in progress."

One night, the Orsers were getting their daughters ready for bed when Myles ran into the bedroom and jumped onto a rocking chair. As the couple helped the toddlers change into their pajamas, Myles seized Norah's discarded pants and raced to his crate.

"I knew he had grabbed something, but I couldn't tell what it was," said Cassandra. "He had only been in his crate for a few seconds, but by the time I got there, he had swallowed something. I checked inside his mouth and in his crate for clues, but I couldn't find anything."

Later that night, neither Cassandra nor Matthew could find Norah's pants anywhere in the house. "All signs pointed to Myles, but we didn't think it was even possible for him to swallow something that large in that short period of time," said Cassandra. "We kept an eye on him just in case, but he acted like his normal self until nearly a week later."

Days after eating the pants, Myles began vomiting. He was getting sicker, so the couple brought him to Arlington Animal Hospital. X-rays of Myles's stomach showed a large blockage in the pooch's intestines, which meant he needed surgery to survive. "It was definitely a scary time," said Cassandra. "We knew he had eaten something, but we still weren't convinced it was the pants."

When the operation was over, Cassandra received a text message from the animal clinic, announcing the surgery was a success. The text included a photo of the cause of the stomach blockage—Norah's missing pants. Remarkably, they were still completely whole without any tears or rips. The veterinary staff washed the pants and returned them to the Orsers when they came to pick up Myles, who made a full recovery.

"Seeing the pants, we were in disbelief," Cassandra told the *Poughkeepsie Journal*. "He swallowed them whole. Not even a nibble!" Now he's too big for his own britches.

ABOUT THE AUTHOR

Allan Zullo is the author of more than 120 nonfiction books on subjects ranging from sports and the supernatural to history and animals.

He has written the bestselling Haunted Kids series, published by Scholastic, which is filled with chilling stories based on, or inspired by, documented cases from the files of ghost hunters. Allan also has introduced Scholastic readers to the Ten True Tales series, about people who have met the challenges of dangerous, sometimes life-threatening situations.

As an animal lover, he is the author of such books as *The Dog Who Saved Christmas and Other True Animal Tales*; *The Dog Who Saved Halloween and Other True Animal Tales*; *Bad Pets Save Christmas*; *Bad Pets Hall of Shame*; *Bad Pets Most Wanted!*; *Bad Pets on the Loose!*; *Bad Pets: True Tales of Misbehaving Animals*; *Miracle Pets: True Tales of Courage and Survival*; *Incredible Dogs and Their Incredible Tales*; *True Tales of Animal Heroes*; and *Surviving Sharks and Other Dangerous Creatures*.

Allan, the grandfather of five and the father of two daughters, lives near Asheville, North Carolina. To learn more about the author, visit his website at www.allanzullo.com.